ESCAPE FROM
HELL

JONATHAN CHRISTOPHERSON

authorHOUSE®

AuthorHouse™
1663 Liberty Drive
Bloomington, IN 47403
www.authorhouse.com
Phone: 1 (800) 839-8640

© 2019 Jonathan Christopherson. All rights reserved.

No part of this book may be reproduced, stored in a retrieval system, or transmitted by any means without the written permission of the author.

Published by AuthorHouse 12/04/2018

ISBN: 978-1-5462-7146-8 (sc)
ISBN: 978-1-5462-7145-1 (e)

Print information available on the last page.

Any people depicted in stock imagery provided by Getty Images are models, and such images are being used for illustrative purposes only. Certain stock imagery © Getty Images.

This book is printed on acid-free paper.

Because of the dynamic nature of the Internet, any web addresses or links contained in this book may have changed since publication and may no longer be valid. The views expressed in this work are solely those of the author and do not necessarily reflect the views of the publisher, and the publisher hereby disclaims any responsibility for them.

This is the story of my experiences in Vietnam. I was a prisoner of war, which you will read about below. I joined the army on July 13, 1966, and I had my basic training at Fort Knox, Kentucky, where I was taught to do hand-to-hand combat and to fire several different weapons—the M60 and the .50-caliber machine gun. I received marksman in shooting. I was also trained to survive anything we might encounter in combat. My advanced training in Fort Sill, Oklahoma, was artillery on a 155 howitzer, which is the size of an army tank but a little bigger and fires a ninety-seven-pound round from a barrel as large as a mechanized cannon. After all my training was complete, we got a thirty-day leave to go home. When I got home, I got married and went to Florida for my honeymoon. After I got back from Florida, I received a plane ticket and a letter with my new orders to report to the military headquarters in Oakland, California. It was a night flight, so I called my folks and told them goodbye and what was going on. I also told my wife's mother goodbye. Brenda, my wife, drove to the airport, and I flew out to Los Angeles, California, where I caught a bus to the army headquarters in Oakland. I got off the bus and had to first go to the check-in quarters, where I was sent to a medical building. I got shots in my arms to protect me from the diseases in Vietnam. After we received our medical clearance, they sent me to another building for supplies. I received my jungle clothing, jungle boots, and a duffel bag to carry my equipment and gear. We were going back to check-in when they told me to go to the food center to eat. It was great food—a hamburger and fries, with a malt to drink. After eating, we were sent to the check-in again, but this time to get loaded onto a cargo plane. They were loading two jeeps and a lot of machine guns and supplies. Thirty-seven soldiers were loaded onto the plane, including me. We were told we were flying to Ton Son Nhut Airfield in South Vietnam, below Saigon. We taxied to the runway and flew out in twenty minutes. There was not a whole lot of room on this plane. I sat on the floor, leaning against the inner wall of the plane. There was no way to see out; it was like flying blind. The only noise was the engine. I fell asleep, and when I woke up we just talked to each other to pass the time. We landed briefly on Wake Island, where we got fuel for the plane, used the restaurant, and stretched our legs until takeoff two hours later. We had a very nice time there. We got some snacks and a drink. I had a good old Coca-Cola. They told us to load back up because we were flying out, so we did. We headed for Ton Son Nhut Airfield. It was nighttime. They said we would be flying in two hours. They were under attack, so the plane would not stop. It slowed to about fifteen miles per hour. The back door of the plane dropped, and we jumped out. The plane took off again. We grabbed our gear, jumped out, and found a place to hide. The jeeps and the crates came off too. We did not hide long before when we went to join the battle. I raised my head to see where I was needed, and that's where I went. Hell, it was my birthday—January 15, 1967—the day we landed. Right away, I had no choice. I went up to the front, where I was needed, and I was scared to kill someone. But when I saw the soldier next to me die, I changed my mind. It was quite a battle. None of the enemy had crossed the barbwire, and the base held them off. I fired at them. I could see they were like ants trying to cross over. There were so many of them that the battle went on for about six hours. When the battle came to an end, the hard part started. They had to go out there and count bodies and see if any were alive. They found a few alive, but badly wounded. There were some wounded, so we took them inside to the medical unit. As new guys, we were very lucky to still be alive. Ton Son Nhut was a good-sized place. It still could have been overrun like anywhere else. We were told to return to the airfield. I went back and found someone to get my orders.

I found a sergeant there who told me that it would be morning before I would have to be there. A man took me over to the barracks. I got something to eat, slept, and walked around until I received my assignment the following morning. All the new guys were there too. We got our assignments. They called my name and said I was assigned to the Third Battalion of the Thirteenth Artillery—Cu Chi. The trucks didn't leave for about four hours, so I just hung out until then. They called us up to load into the trucks. I got in the truck going to

Cu Chi. The trucks started to leave. There were two trucks going to Cu Chi. We were sent with the Third and Fourth Cav and the Fifth Meck, who led us there. The other truck came with us. We took Highway 1 to Cu Chi. It did not take a long time to get down the road. Cu Chi was not all that big, but there was a lot there. We got off the truck at the headquarters. We were escorted to the Third Battalion of the Thirteenth Artillery. I was told to go over to gun number one, so I did. I met the sergeant in charge of the gun. He was the gunner, and there was also Harold, Red, and another, but I do not remember his name. The sergeant told me I was the ammo man, hauling ninety-seven-pound shells to the gun. The sergeant said we would just hang around the gun until we got a fire mission, so I learned to do that really well. The Third of Thirteenth was on the west side of Cu Chi. It was like a little compound of our own, but we were in Cu Chi. There was not much going on there. We didn't have any work to do, so we just hung around the gun like the sergeant said. The gun had a .50-caliber machine gun on top, and the sergeant assigned me to that at night for guard. Our unit had six 155 howitzers, a mess truck, an ammo truck, and a jeep. That's all of it. We were artillery, but we acted like infantry if needed. The sergeant said we would leave for Tribee in two days, just north of us. The headquarters sent a message to us to fire six rounds at seven charges. They would pound poles into the ground of each track. They used those to set quadrant and deflection and set the height of the barrel. We fired the mission they gave us, and then we just hung around. We packed up everything for the trip to Tribee, loaded rounds and powder onto the truck, and got the mess truck ready. The mess truck was like a portable restaurant. The field major, captain, and lieutenant were on the jeep. None of the officers wore any insignia. That was an army regulation in Vietnam. We headed for our destination. The number one and number two trucks led the way, then the ammo truck, followed by the number three and the number four trucks next, then the mess truck, then the number five and number six trucks, and the jeep last. The gunners on the trucks sat outside, ready to fire rounds if needed. I was on top of the truck, ready to use the .50-caliber machine gun. We were traveling along Highway 1. On the way to Tribee, we passed four villages and saw the villagers. They looked like nice people. We were getting close to Tribee—about five miles to go. They said it was quite a small compound. We pulled into a big tent. The barracks were about sixty feet wide and two stories high. There was a cooking station, a bathroom, and a couple jeeps. We were led to where we could set up the trucks, ammo, and mess truck. After the trucks were in place, the ammo truck drove around to each truck. The crews on each truck unloaded their rounds and powder. We were all set up when we got a mission—three rounds, charge seven.

The captain came over and said we had done a good job. This place did not feel right. I had a feeling the Vietnamese soldiers didn't like us very much. We got a mission. The six guns were setting up for a long-distance fire. I brought the round to the back of the gun and handed it to the number one man, who took it and screwed a timer on top of the shell. He set the time it would detonate. He shoved it in the barrel and then put in the powder. He closed the breach bloke, put in an igniter, and then pulled the cord. The round was fired. On the end of the barrel there was a flash compressor that allowed the barrel concussion out both sides of the barrel. Between each round that was fired, I ran with a shell to the back of the truck. That way, I was not caught by the concussion from the barrel. After five rounds were fired, we were done. The sergeant said for me to pick up the shell casings, set them beside the ammo bunker, and bring five rounds to the back of the gun so we were ready for another mission. I then had to get back on the machine gun. The other guys are in there jobs, everything is running smooth, and good. We are going to eat, each crew goes to eat, and they return another one goes. We have bunkers we built for Guard duties by each gun. The guys are digging holes in the ground for toilets we bring two halves of a fifty-gallon drum with us in the tracks we place them in the holes and lay boards over the top to sit on.

We are getting close to midafternoon and everything is real quiet. The Sergeant is concerned of how quiet it is here with so many Vietnam Army, which are Vietnamese soldiers. It doesn't seem right, so the sergeant is going over to the major's tent to see what he thinks about it. The Sergeant came back and said the major is going to talk to the Arvin major. They're getting ready to go out to Monkey Mountain for a search and destroy mission. We are really going to watch the ones that stay behind because the major thinks that the Cong are going to attack us and take over and then attack the Vietnamese Arvin from the back. The Commander of the Arvin told our major that there was radio that the Cong were spotted not far from the compound about ten miles, with all of the bunkers done and really settled in we have the 3/4th Cav and 5th Mech are going to be here in about four hours after bring us here they went on to somewhere and are returning soon. We have started on some ditches the major decided we need they will be 6' long and 4' deep by 4' these are where we can have the other men in. We have help from the Vietnamese soldiers that were left here so that's a big help. What is different about them helping is you don't know if they can be trusted or not.

The Infantry is not here yet, now that work is done we are having super and just relaxing night. We are going to play cards tonight, that's going to be a lot of fun, we play for the ciggs from the sea rations we eat. Every ration has four ciggs in each one. I don't smoke so I just give mine to the losers anyway. We get packages in the mail occasionally from home, I haven't yet. The guys get some pretty neat stuff, Bill got a cassette player and a few of the rock in roll cassettes and with fresh batteries and when we play cards he's going to play them. We got some three two beers from the Arvin's and so that's nice. We are playing cards and I have no luck at all I've lost four in hands in a row. Harold the Sergeant has lit up some cigar and having a blast while the music from the cassette player beach boys, Letterman, and Roy Robinson, it is so cool.

The guys are having a good time. I got real tired and went to get some sleep, it's about three AM and everything is great so far. The 5th Mech just showed up, hell I can't sleep anyway so I'm getting up and relieved one of the men on Guard duty. It's morning and we are having breakfast, eggs **powdered** and toast and coffee good stuff. We are just sitting around enjoying the hot weather hugely jungle and watching the sweat roll of like rain. It's in the hundreds and not even noon yet. I look like it might rain today. It's clouding up pretty good. I hope it does it cool things off, but if it rains tonight so it won't be good on Guard duty. It's about 11 AM and we are doing some different things. The Sergeant asked us to do, it's now three PM after the Guard duties so I was sent back to the track and told to get on the 50-up top, and to keep my eyes open for any sound of trouble. I'm using binoculars, I can see a lot from here. Not much fun in the hot sun where the rain is. The Sergeant got information from the captain that there are Cong moving our way, the air force was called to strike with napalm bombs and we will see what happens after that.

The 3/4th Cave and 5th Mech are moving out in the direction of the Cong with the napalm, which should kill off a bunch if they spot them. We are on full alert, just the same. We are hoping the Cong do not show up here. The captain is wired that if they do, it may be tough with all the new replacements we have. The attack is not what I am looking forward to mc because I'm new myself. It is starting to rain and if they attack tonight with it raining, there better in that than we are because they are very well used to it. It is now getting dark and still raining harder. It is ten PM and I'm on the 50 on top getting wet more than ever. I've got the 50 covered with a cover made from tarp, over in the middle of the compound on the edge of the bunker and there is a Vietnamese Soldier just sitting there and not even talking. When asked something, that's strange. There are Vietnamese Soldiers with their guns staring at us, there right where one of the bunkers are at over on the other side of the compound. The sergeant on gun three spotted some lights across the rice paddy and we looked and yes, but there was a Vietcong kneeling down on his knees with a flash light and every time he flashes the flash light a light comes on, that is a mortar platoon, which yes know there fixing to mortar us.

One of the Vietnamese Soldiers is sneaking up on the guy with the flash light, he grabbed him from the back and cut his throat. We are getting mortared right now one after another. I'm off the top and headed to the bunker. Explosions are all over and we are in deep trouble. We are catching fire from the Arvin barrack and everybody is headed for cover. The mortars are coming in on us, and fire from receiving fire from the barracks. Apparently the ones in the barrack are Cong.

We are getting attacked, we are holding on pretty good so far, but still fighting hard to stay alive, I don't know how I got into the Compound without any body seeing, but they did and now we are in battle up to our ears a couple of the guys got hit and are down. I'm pulling one of them to cover. There are one of the guys that didn't make it. He's dead. We did not grab him because we don't have time. The Sergeant is yelling at one to get on the 50 calibers. I'm a shooting target up here. I'm firing at the perimeter trying to do the best I can to kill a lot of them. They are coming like flies. All the 50s are firing and the guys up front doing good with their M60's. The Cong are dropping like mosquitos being spayed. It's not something to think about killing them, you just do. We are in bad shape, there are Cong coming out of the barracks and now they are in the Compound. They are all over now and I can't fire the 50 without killing our own. I'm off the track in hand to hand Combat. One is running right at me and I fired a few into him but he is still running at me. Harold just knocked him down with his M16 machine gun and yelled, "Get with the battle, don't be afraid!"

I got up off the ground and attacked. Been doing good but they are using machine guns and with bayonets attached to them. God, *it's a mad house here there is so many of them.* The Arvin Commander just got shot. Our Major and Captain fell to the rear. The 5th Mech are here now they came in from behind the Cong so now they're boxed in our Infantry is coming from all around the barrack and now we are really kicking ass. I'm bashing one's head and there is one coming up behind me. I turned and shoved my M16 in his gut and knocked him down and shot him. Now there's another, he's running with his bayonet. I just turned and shot him. It went on like this four better part of another two hours. It is starting to let up and a lot of the Cong are dead, a few of us as well. The battle caused my mind to flip out and I'm screaming and yelling, *Lord what have you done*!

The rain is still raining hard and you know it's day light by about two hours. There were a lot captured by the Infantry and were taken to the center of the compound and held there until the body count was done. Medical choppers have been called to pick up the wounded and choppers were coming in to pick up the dead. We are loading them up now and they have taken off to wherever they go. We have a lot of cleanup to do and a lot to prepare for whatever comes up.

After it took us three days to clean the place up and the Army engineers came in from somewhere, don't know for sure because I don't ask I just do whatever I'm told to do. We're eating and just sitting around I'm thinking of telling you this. Weeks have gone by, the Soldiers that were out on the mission are coming back in from the mountain. The report was, they did not run in to the Cong at all pretty peculiar that they went out and found none. We get them all here and then after the battle. they come back in. We are getting everything to move out to just South of Pliyku. It's quite a way from here we are again on highway number one road of Vietnam ha. We need to be there in four days, so we are moving as usual. It's now in to February, we really hope it's a better month. These memories are a lot to live with. I feel like I got run over with a track. I'm sore all over I'll get better as time goes by. We are crossing over east off the highway. Itt's not much of a road its like running threw a rice paddy with lots of water and mud were running on the outside of the jungle. It seems we cannot move as fast as we did on the highway.

The 5th Mech are with us after we get to where we are going. They will leave us. One of the Infantry told me they have business to take care of us. We are passing some small villages, they're so small, the hooch's look like extra big Dog houses. We are stopping to set up lunch and check our supplies. It's been night and day we had to get moving so we are now going through some jungle, not very thick you can see a lot. It's mostly trees and brush. There is a village we are passing the major decided we should spend the night here and leave out in the morning for the rest of the way. We are set up in a zigzag with the tracks sort of guarding the Majors jeep and him setting up alongside the jeep. we will pull half Guard and switch every four hours. The Guard is handling the 50s on top the track, all of the others are getting some sleep and some are smoking and just relaxing, I'm going to relieve the Guard it's almost five AM, so it won't be very long before we get packed to move out. Harold just asked me about back home, he is telling me about his wife and children, he misses kids' smile every morning. Pretty cool about his camera and all sorts of things about what school he went to, etc. I told him about the great looking wife I have back home. She is so great to be around and that she is finishing another year of college while I'm here, etc. It's good to talk about the good things. It makes being here a little better in a certain way - yes know what I mean.

The first lieutenant is sick, they're calling a medical chopper with a medic to check him out, the lieutenant looks really bad, after that battle we had, he seemed like something was wrong with him sense then but getting worse, we are running out of food, we will just cut down off eating regular and have two meals per day instead of the three until the chopper brings more plus brings up more ammo for the machine guns we are running low on them. They have been notified from the captain, so it should not be a couple of days to get them. I'm cleaning off the 50 on top, it got wet and is dirty. The captain noticed when he was walking by and got sort of angry at the filthy gun and chewed me out for not keeping it clean, hell what does he expect, we didn't have time to clean it tell now, and because I didn't have the gun clean, he is making me clean inside the track as well. Everyone else now are cleaning their guns after hearing the captain chewed me out. Now everyone has got a bad attitude. Every gun is cleaned already except the 50s, but he's making us clean them all again, maybe he is sick too ha-ha. Now that is done. Red is over to track four trying to convince the Sergeant to play cards with us later, he's a sucker for cards. It's the first week of February, it sure seemed like we have been in this way longer than we have, the days are slow here only the Major has a watch.

He surely would not tell us what time it is, so we just guess. It is not like the Rambo movie where everyone has watches ha-ha. We just get word of a mission so we are setting up. I'm getting rounds and red is getting the powder, Harold the Sergeant just said five rounds, seven charge continuous then we will wait ½ hour and do it again, Red is getting in the back to fire the rounds. He's is the #one man that fires them, the Sergeant is calling deflection and Amad is calling quadrant. Those are direction and height of the barrel.

Weave fired the first mission and setting up for the next. The Infantry out there in the woods are trying to flush the Cong out with grenades but it's not working so we are firing just passed where they think they are. If they don't run out we will drop them right on the spot the Infantry thinks they are. On the second mission, Red got his hand bruised by the breach block, but he is still firing. God that must really hurt, we were going to trade places, but he said "No, I'll do it" and he did it. The mission is over and I'm collecting the mess up. We're going to get food by gun first #6 then #5 and so on.

Harold and red are my best friends out here and we really do look out for each other. We got to nam at the same time and went through hell together. We still call ourselves rookies just for fun. We are ready to move out when we get the word, it's quiet. There's a few Vietnamese watching us and some kids wanting candy. We were trained in the States about this, kids get the candy take it to their moms and they in turn get the candy to the Cong which in turn inject poison in them, give the candy back to the village, and in turn try and give candy back to the Soldiers. We are not allowed to give or take candy, but some Soldiers do. The people back home think that the kids are the innocent ones, but that is far from right. The people back home call us baby killers well they're not here.

We are moving out now, the 5th Mech is in front, two tracks, the jeep, mess truck two trucks, the ammo truck, two more tracks, we only move slow threw this mud but we're moving, we are moving by a village, pretty good size four hutches and a lot of little shacks made out of bamboo, they are waving, and we are waving back. They seem friendly and that is nice for a change. Riding on top the track is like a Bull in a rodeo. Sometimes yes get bounced up and down its pretty rough on the spin but I can't complain, it's better out here than in the track. The kids are trying to give us candy now we know that there are Cong in that village, but yes can't tell which ones, they all where silk clothes. We are getting fired at from the village and we have stopped and are firing into it all the villagers are running around, we don't know who is, but we are firing any way cause if we take fire we give fire and I know some die for nothing.

We have a cease fire, the 5th Mech are driving into the village and deploying out of the military trucks and search and destroy. There are going in there with ten Soldiers and everything is silent apparently most everyone in the village is either dead or ran off. Yes there were women and children, but we can't blame ourselves because we got fired upon. It happens a lot when those stupid idiots but there children at risk. The 5th Mech captured three that were apparently Cong, one woman and two children survived the mess. They are questioning the people and they did find a tunnel underneath a cooking pot, *I can't believe it, they are cooking Dog!* They eat dogs like we eat ham, the 5th Mech radioed back to the base that they had prisoners there going to turn them over to an Arvin chopper in a bit. We are moving out to our destination we are about 8 miles from there, just south of here along the Cambodian border, just south from Pliyku and then straight east to the boarder. We are told that there are tunnels all around Cu Chi, Tri bee, Saigon, Ton son Nhut, other places that always a danger when traveling anywhere in the south Vietnam.

When we get to our place of destination, they choppers will fly in with our supplies. We will be getting a small one eight cannons that tows behind a truck or jeep. The cannon will be able to counter act mortar attacks, a shot just went off in our group or one of the tracks, it sound like an M16 rifle, yes it was the Sergeant said one of the guys on truck four shot himself in the leg on top the truck with the guy on the 50 caliber having this other guy on the truck riding up there with the M16 pointed at his leg. They hit a bump and the gun went off. Now we are stopped, and everybody is just looking at the track, things happen but was it done on purpose or not. Either way he's going home. We can't say a word because we will never no. When we stop again we will be setting up right away for missions. The Sergeant says we won't get any sleep for a while longer, hell we've been up now for twenty hours now, just great!

As traveling we see Vietnamese working there rice paddies on the right and on the left is just a lot of jungle. The Vietnamese are loading there baskets and then loading on wagons that are pulled by hand. It's a nice day weather wise. Temperature is around 110 degrees kinda hot, but not like it was. Some of the Vietnamese just stare at us, you never know if they are counting how many of us there are and what kinda fire power we have. You can often sense a Cong by the way they act, yes never know if there are snipers in the jungle to out left or what is going on with the Vietnamese in the paddy's we be afraid 24-7. We on the 50's is a real good target. I volunteered for Vietnam so it's my fault I'm in the hell. We are now pulling into our place of detention ha ha-ha. It's pretty nice compared from before, it solid ground and cleaned out pretty good.

There are Infantry here some of the 100 and first Airborne that were chopperd in here. They are leading us in to where they would like us to set up. We are set up in like a half circle and the jeep with the cannon are set up in the middle. The Army engineers plowed all the jungle out and leveled it off so it's good hard surface, it's great for the trucks. There's still some work to be done, but we are going to fire first. Mission is ten rounds per gun, quadrant + deflection is set, red is lunching the first round and placing in the powder, sitting in the igniter and firing one and the rest the same way the timer on top the rounds. I've already screwed them on and set the time. Nine rounds have been fired and the last one in going in and now fired we're done, now we just wait for radio confirmation on what the rounds did. The Cong were at this point according to the radio report and we managed to put them to rest on attacking the Infantry, the Cong are scattered all over, great and good news, we did it. Now were cleaning up the truck and getting ready for another one, this mission just had caught the Cong coming in across the border and into Vietnam with supplies and guns and ammo, we got them after they entered, we had to wait until they were in Vietnam because we aren't allowed to fire into Cambodia.

After the Infantry goes in that area they should not have much resistance, were told to stay close to the guns in case they need us. We just got word that the Cong destroyed a village just south of Saigon about mid-way between Saigon and Ton son Nhut Air base. The Infantry wasn't even close to them, that's sad when they kill their own. Apparently, they were fighting back and did not survive. I just cannot believe who we are fighting, like I said before they all look alike. A lot look at us like we do not belong here, and you get people that really care about us, figure that out.

When we get shots from a village that's the worst time of my life, thinking just who we really killed. Good, bad, and the hugely hard core from North Vietnam. We've been here a couple of weeks now and we are getting ready to move out of here. It's nice here I wish we could stay a lot longer. We are moving south that's all I know, we first have to burn the tubs and undig them and put them on the ammo truck and take the shower down, then pick up everything and move, and guess who has to burn the tubs, good old me as usual, you would listen to my complaints and let someone else do that for a change. I guess I do them so well ha hahaha. We move out with just the rounds in our tracks the rest mount on the truck. When we get to our location Ammo trucks will come up and supplies us with a lot of rounds and powder, along with ammo for our machine guns I hate that because everything must be taken care of by hand. We just get lunch and it was not sea rations, it is sausage and eggs, nice, very nice. We are on the move now as regular and we are moving over land south west of where we are at. It's the 27th of February, just about to the end, one day ha. We just found out we are going back to Cu Chi, isn't that great, just think food, beer, what could be better than that. The guns have a deal that for whatever reason if one gun fires we all do, I think I have mentioned that before. That's to get the upperhand on whatever is going on. It's good we have a better chance to go home.

When I first got here the first battle, I was scared to kill someone, but now, it's a means of life, and I don't think twice about it, that's a fact and I stick by it like a glove. We are stopping in just about one hour and pulling off into a small Arvin Compound to get sleep and get our self's ready for the rest of the trip. The Sergeant says we are taking a different route back, this should be interesting, the sun is out and it's a pretty hot day in the above a 100 mark.

It's so hot the Sergeant gave me a blanket to but under my butt because the metal is so darn hot and I have a cover for my gun. The Sergeant says on the way back we will be stopping at a good size village and we are not allowed to go in there for our own safety. I guess he knows what he's saying. We are at the village, and we get word the Infantry is being pinned down about two miles from where we are, so we are spreading the tracks out and awaiting word on where to fire and how many. We are working with only the rounds in the truck to work with because we don't have time to get Ammo off the truck we've got enough for ten rounds that's per truck so that is plenty. No mission yet but we are ready just sitting here waiting for the word but still nothing yet. We get the word three rounds one and one-half mile for affect. The Sergeant says we are done with the mission and the Infantry is getting the small group left of the Cong head on and doing a great job. We now pack up and get sleep and food for the night and move back to Cu Chi in the morning. Figures in a couple hours we will be back in Cu Chi. That's the best idea we've had all day ha. Now we are back sitting into our regular places for the trucks and I'm already on

Guard duty for tonight, that's no problem, it must be done, I like Guard duty, the compound had two mortar attacks sense we were gone and the Commander of the Compound told our Major that he would like it if we could have a couple of men outside the perimeter and about seven hundred meters with radios. The major told the Sergeant to pick one man per gun to report to the major. I was one that was picked, *why me?* The Sergeant said just do what you're told and have no nonsense, oh I said, so I reported to the Major. The Major said me and Bruce were to go out outside of our perimeter of the tracks, cool. We don't go out there now only when it gets just about dark. Me and Bruce decided that when we go out Bruce will have the M60 machine gun and I'll have the radio and my M16 machine gun. We are just now obeying the orders the Major gave us and moving out the compound, it's quite a way out, and dark we are about where they want us, and setting up the machine gun on its holder.

We are set now radioing back to the Compound that we are set. They told us that if any lights are seen out here to radio in immediately and if they get close to open up fire on them right away and then get our butts back fast. The base has a fire mission we were told so we'll hear rounds over us they make quite a noise when they are fired in back of us, we are just watching for flashlights out here and I think to myself if we see flash light facing us then we could be seen really easy, we see nobody and see no light so far and it's about two AM.

We do hear movement but see nothing, it could just be a dog or pig or some other kind of animal, still don't see a thing I radioed in and told them we hear something out here but do not see anything moving. They said if it keeps up fire a few and see what happens. I said no we are not giving out where we are, unless we see something and he said do as you're told. We quite talking to them, to give position away is pure stupid. The Infantry called Compound and said they need some rounds out there they are in deep blank and need them now, the guns are firing out into the jungle part of where the Infantry are, we are still here, we are hoping the Infantry are doing OK, were looking for anything that moves or lights, nothing yet but I 'am scared being out here so far and a long way to run if we have to. We have no Idea how the Infantry is doing just hoping like hell they kick the Congs butt big time. Butch just said in whisper very low voice that there is something out there and it doesn't sound like a small animal, we're very hard to see something but still don't. He called back, and they said some

Infantry is coming out where we are and to not get scared when they get there because there ours.

There they are there going further out, they just found an old Vietnamese man just walking around out there they took him in to custody and taking back to the post. We are still left here. They took the old man right away back we found out later that he was a Cong spying on us to report back to the Cong what he saw like ammo and equipment that we have so they could figure out how to attack and where. They delivered him to the Commander for questioning to find out where the Cong are, Butch has got good ears. They turned the old man over to the Arvin here and let them find out, The Arvin torture them an awful lot to find out something and a lot of the time and then they shot them and for some God forsaken things the Americans can't do a Darn thing about it. The Air force was called in to napalm the area the Cong were supposed to be you can hear the jets coming over us, what a sound we can see by the fire out there that spreads all across the jungle that napalm burns them up like an incinerator nothing left but skeleton powder. We saw once when we were in a position just short of a large field and we were firing on Cong crossing the field there was quite a bunch of them the Air force jets came over us and dropped napalm on the field one big flame that went across the field and all we saw after it was done was a lot of smoke, they were burned so bad you could hardly see the bone.

We were called back to camp, and we had a mission I was number one man I was the one shoving the rounds in the barrel and that seats the round then I put the powder in set the igniter and pulled the lanyard and the rounds were off, six in a row, then we were done nothing to do but pray the rounds did some good for the Infantry, we are again cleaning the guns and getting them ready for the next one we have to fire. We have to check the flash compressor to see that there is no damage, it looks good, sometimes if we fire a lot of missions the flash compressor is a little melting and that is bad news, so we check it out from time to time. Sergeant said get shower and clean up our weapons after. The lieutenant is getting on our nerves with his state side manners he acts like he just got out of military school.

The lunch is coming up and man I am very hungry, we are hoping that we get something besides sea rations. We are moving out of here in one day some were by a rice paddy on one side and jungle on the other sounds familiar about where we were once before. We are moving now we have about ten miles from here, and up highway number one it's so dry that the dust is blinding us usually is a little muddy but not this trip. The Sergeant says we will be there in one day, I can see that it's only ten miles, we are five miles short of the destination not bad we are making good time, and we will be there in about one hour, cool we are looking forward to stopping after this bumpy ride. The Major told the captain that we will be coming to a little village that is only a quarter mile from where we will be at and they have had Cong going through the village about two days ago, we stopped just short of the village and the Sergeants were told to keep a very good eye out might be some Cong in the area, so now we are moving right by the village and it looks normal to me, but we are looking around the village to see if anyone or a few Vietnamese are in a group that could be Cong, but like I said before they all look alike so who is who. Any way there is nothing to bother us, so we are just pulling into our destination, there is a field in front of us it's tall grass of some kind which is a perfect spot to hide Vietcong, There is Infantry nearby, we first have to build bunkers for the ammo and then build Guard bunkers, so we parked the guns where the captain said and we are building the bunkers we have a bunch of sand bags that were in the back of the truck so we are filling them with dirt and pilling them up for the bunkers we have boards that are placed on top and then we put sand bags on top.

After seeing what they do to the Infantry we have no remorse for whatever the Infantry does to them. It's now midnight and all is well in the big city, we are on Guard, but we are talking back home and relaxing and keep our eyes open we know that if we see or hear anything out there we are prepared for anything we are switching Guards now and I get some sleep which I am ready for. Red said you guys should be more into the War instead of so much fun, he's gone wacko we are but dog gone we need some fun to, he as just got a bad attitude right, but he'll come back around. Going to have a mission finally, we've been here two weeks without one, it's small just six rounds charge six, and we finished and found out that it was scare tactic where the Cong was starting to come together into a bunch, so we messed that up. Do gone it we are going to move in the second morning from here, time to move I'm back up top with my friend the 50 were moving out, the Sergeant made a joke, we are leaving to beat the traffic. It's in a way true because the Cong do not attack so much during the day, usually late day or night. It's about mid-February close one day away from March.

We are headed to base camp, that will be great, for one reason, to refresh the trucks and the equipment and for the second reason for some beer, it's just three two beer but it is sure good, we are on our way along this jungle road we've gone passed the village and it was OK it's actually a nice village with some nice people very friendly and nice to us this time, we're about two miles from the village and the jeep got a flat. We are stopped until it's fixed it's the major jeep so OK we would not leave him behind hahaha. I'm always nervous when we are just sitting still on the road, the weather has cooled off to about ninety degrees, and cloudy all of us are on full alert just stopped here is a real target at our tracks being so large. Jeep is fixed and were moving, we don't have far to go were only three miles from Cu Chi. Red came up and replaced me on the 50 until we get home yes, it is, at least well we are here. The Sergeant well we are back let's get in and park these beasts and get some beer I said to the Sergeant I'm going out to get a shower and eat then I'll go for some beer, he said whatever because we are free to leave the tracks for the rest of the day. He's telling us do and go anywhere in the Compound tell six PM and then we must be back for supper and Guard duty so after my shower me and Red went into the bigger part of the camp to check it out, there is a small hooch that you can drink beer in and hear some good music, it's a cool place.

We just got word everyone is now on alert for battle if necessary, so we are running back to the track and getting orders from the Major. He said according to the camp commander that an Air Force spotter plane flying over Saigon spotted a large group of Hard core Cong from the north approaching us threw Saigon on an attempt to attack the Compound, to me those Cong are assholes with brains of stone. We are setting up all the fire power the Infantry here have and it's a lot there setting up at the far end of Cu Chi facing Saigon. Darn we just got word that the Cong aren't going to attack the compound cause according to the radio from the spotter plane is that they are pulling away from the other side of Saigon and headed south toward Ton son Nhut Air force base, there word that the 100 and first Air borne are flying in on quite a few choppers to drop in on those Cong and attack them that's very cool, that means we will have fire missions to help, the major got word from the base commander to move our tracks to east west north and south in the camp and after we get moved to set up and fire one round every ten minutes close range of the Compound in case the Cong change their minds and do decide to attack us in that case if we were to be mortared before an attack they at least would not hit the ammo and powder that we have all at once.

If they fire rockets at the tracks we are not bunched up in one location which is real good thinking of the camp commander. With the Infantry and all of us set up for battle we just sit and hope the Cong did move south it's two AM and the infantry is sending up flares which are great for seeing anybody out there. If anything is seen moving around out there we can open fire immediately and then continue the flares so the Cong light up like a candle. It's four AM and we have nothing moving at all, and we've seen no lights for setting up mortars so we are all cool, It would be to close for firing our guns and we with our guys are not going to go out there like the Infantry can, so we just man the 50's and other machine guns we have.

We are getting fire mission for all the tracks firing the rounds south east of Saigon continuous fire about a mile out from the camp I'm caring two rounds on my shoulder and one across my neck each time I get the rounds they guys on the ammo bunker load me like that every time I go and get the ammo. It seems pretty easy when your six ft. tall weight two thirty-five and built like a bull like I said it's easy, we are five rounds fired so far and being continuous fire, it could be any amount until the flash compressor gets real red then we must stop before it melts. The hundred and first is out there kicking their butts and we are firing exactly where they want them, so we hope the best for them.

They have called off the guns for now so we are taking turns to shower + eat, now they have me on Guard duty in the bunker and getting some sleep while red is on Guard it's eleven am and so far we've heard nothing to say mission pulling Guard even if were all over the Compound because the Infantry have been doing a lot of Guard duty while we were gone, switching every four hours it's my turn to replace red. It's now one pm all the guys of ours are off Guard duty and we are going to tell rick that the Major wants to see him, we found out that he's going home, his father has passed away and he is the only child so he's being sent home and getting out of the army to take care of his mother, that's pretty sad I would not want to be in his shoes going home to bury his father. He's going to get choppers out for Tonsonut Air field to catch a flite home. Glad he's going, but very sad about why he's going.

There is Vietnamese outside the compound just walking around asking Soldiers if they can do our laundry and other things the Major of the whole compound is telling the men to not let them in the compound, they can talk to us outside of the compound but that's it. We are told to get in the bunker and get the machine guns in place to fire. It's now been quite a day, but the day is about over it is now gone to evening and there is some alert they put us on so I'm in the bunker in front of the track. There is four Infantry men stationed outside each bunker, what the hell is going on they won't say because they don't know. It's eleven pm and we have a mission so back out of the bunkers we come. Setting the gun for six rounds as fast as we can fire them toward the direction of Tribee, our Infantry which is our 25th are out there in a bind, they moved into a place they did not know that the Cong almost have them surrounded and we have to give them a little help so we are starting we are to fire now fast as we can, they are in a lite bind hope we can get them free to battle right, there getting mortared along with getting shot at. The battle they tell us is getting worse weave changed direction and we are still firing none stop. The battle the 25th Infantry won that one with the air force leading them a hand and now later the 25th are in trouble this is two battles in two weeks, choppers have shown up to get the Infantry here the choppers have machine guns attached to the door of the choppers so they will do really well from the air after dropping the Infantry we are still firing now a different direction again our flash compressors are starting to glow we've got to stop before they melt, sorry for the Infantry but we have to wait until the glow goes down to where we can fire again. The choppers set the Infantry right in with the rest and the choppers are peppering the Cong with their door machine guns hoping they don't get shot down.

Quite a battle out there, but we still can't fire. Got radio connection that they are winning the battle there is a lot of Cong dead and wounded a lot scattered and quite of a few of them were captured, so they did a hell of a good job out there. We found out that the Arvin Soldiers were there as well helping. They are going to take charge of the prisoners and the Infantry will fall back here and fly out the wounded, which they say is a bunch. We are not bothering the tracks right now we are letting them finish cooling off and we will clean them later, I'm burning the toilet pit's and the Sergeant got stuck with cleaning the pots and pans at the mess truck. I can't figure out why in the hell is he's doing that unless he pissed off the captain because that definitely is not the Sergeants job. Harold the Sergeant is my best friend's here we used to pull Guard together, eat together and now he's Sargent and we don't do those together, but we still look out for each other and that is the way it will still be. We are going to leave in a couple of days for monkey mountain just north of Tribee the marines are there planning something that really weird because the marines are usually north around the DMZ that what I was told anyway. I'm done burning the toilets I'm cleaning my M16 machine gun I have to go and get some ammo clips later because I have only got two and we are supposed to have four clips. I have a sore shoulder I think I pulled a muscle. We want to go drink some beer and the Sergeant says go for it, you guys deserve it. Drinking beer, smoking and looking at the ladies is quite a deal, the more you drink the better looking they get ha ha-ha, you could be looking at an old lady and think she looked twenty one, the guys don't trust the Vietnamese ladies after what happened in Saigon where one of our Soldiers took this lady into her hooch to make love and they were making love the other soldiers heard a loud scream, they ran over and saw the guy standing there with his penuse was cut four ways, the woman had a blade mechanism in side her that would split the penuse when he entered and withdrew it sliced him, the guys shot her about thirty times, and got him to medical right away even though that happened he was sent back home for court martial for destroying government property and will get him a dishonorable discharge, what a dump ass he is. See it's not just the male Cong against us it's the females to. It's hard to write this but if it wasn't true I would not write it. You have to know the whole truth about the war from my experience in 1967 nothing has happened sense the battle we are setting everything back to normal and getting duties to do except for breakfast sometime early sometime late but that's the way it goes now meals are different now we get our food and take it back to your position after eating me and red are playing cards that his mother sent him in a care package he opened here in the camp, we get a chance to go to Saigon tomorrow with the Sergeant. We are going to check out the stores there and we can buy, trade etc we are really looking forward to that, we can only be there for four hours but we are only spend two hours so that others may go, guys will be able to go there for the next few days we are back now I got a Vietnamese blanket four a pair of socks, pretty cool isn't it, now we are just hanging out by the truck and drinking some beer and just chilling out. This black guy is cool he's dancing. The Infantry is got supplies that are just delivered from a couple choppers we are watching them unload the supplies, but we have to stay out of there way while there unloading. Well the unloading is done, and the choppers left. The wounded Soldiers we heard are flown to Japan or Germany for medical care and then flown home. Some more Infantry came in with some of them wounded, they must have called ahead for the choppers because they are just flying in they are loading the wounded in the chopper and they are done, the choppers are leaving, there was five of them.

The captain for the Infantry came over to the major and thanked him personally for the support we gave them in the last mission we had and then walked over to the tracks and thanked the Sergeant also, we are all getting ready to eat, the food that was flown in and the Infantry is sharing their food with all of us man is it ever good. A lot better than we have been eating. The fun is just beginning, they will stay here for three days, it won't be no trouble for me and Harold and red to drink beer. It is late into the first night there here and still allowed to party, those guys are really a tough bunch of Soldiers. Darn it I must go burn the drum barrels and have to fill the shower and we can go back and party. I decided I had enough of the party so I'm going back to the track and clean my guns etc. Every day the jobs change and that's good, it's like a card game, it's what hand you are dealt. Well I'm back on Guard duty for only the rest of the night which is only two hours. When I get off Guard duty, we are going to go out around and look for tunnels nothing to do on the track, so the Sergeant is letting me and red go out we will be going we are with the compound Infantry, the Infantry that came here for three days and going to stay here and rest a couple more days.

We are out about one half mile from camp in tall grass, the tunnels can be found any ware around Saigon + Cu Chi, we are walking through the grass looking for little brush piles in the tall grass it's very hard to find, we have to watch where we step and eyes open for Cong popping up and taking a shot. Brush piles are all over Vietnam, that's why the Cong cover there tunnels in some way to make it look like a regular brush pile they don't think that the Infantry will check all brush piles, but they do when they are out just looking for tunnels.

We are spread out about the field the Infantry can cover more territory that way, I see a couple piles I'm kicking them around but there is no tunnels so are the rest, suddenly a guy to the left of us spotted one he is uncovering it the Infantry are all gathering around the tunnel one of them is going down in the tunnel to search, he's called a tunnel rat. He must watch for booby traps that the Cong set up in the tunnels in case we find one, one guy told me that they have booby traps with tripwires strung across inner tunnel and in the wall of the tunnel they have a pocket of scorpions messed over and when the wire is pulled the scorpions fall out on you, there deadly. He has been down there about one-half hour and he is coming out he reported that way in the tunnel he came across an area of weapons, food etc.

The Infantry leader told him to go and set explosive charges in the supplies area and run the wire back and he did, this time we were hoping there were no Cong there yet. He is coming back out with the wire we string it about fifty yards from the tunnel he will ignite the wire and get the hell out of here back to camp, Butch says aren't we going to watch the explosion and the Infantry man said hell no we don't want to be here when that goes off, they ignited it and we are running back toward camp the tunnel exploded it is huge we can feel the ground shake, we got to get back to camp we are on a half run so we will be back in camp in about twenty minutes on the way back we heard a second explosion, the guy said that was not understanding why. We are back, and the Sergeant says, go get some food then go replace the Guard on #3 gun, and get some rest there.

The food is good, and I'll get some sleep. It's toward dark and the other Infantry are going out for a search and destroy mission, only twenty are going out found out that's a platoon, really cool, they will be out for days, but I do not know for who long. It's morning now about six am and I'm off Guard and going to burn the toilets, it's pretty hot out already about one hundred degrees. Artillery is a hard job on hot days it's real tough, and other days it's easy, but artillery never changes. We gone sometimes fifty hours before sleep, and that's if we have a lot of missions in a row and on alert, of possible attack. I started smoking ciggs here in Nam every sea ration comes with four Ciggs per meal, I was giving them away, but one day I was really nervous, and I smoked one I coughed a while, but it made me not be very nervous so I kept on smoking.

I've had breakfast and now I must fill up the shower tubs. I'm done with that and nothing for me to do right now but just hang loose and see what comes up later. I went to get mail because they called mail call, I got a package from home, I opened it and there is a Jare of peanut butter, a picture of mom, dad, and wife, plus a can of chilly, and can of peaches, that is so cool, the picture is of them sitting on the back porch it is so cool seeing my family, it sure made me feel good. I put the picture inside my helmet, that way I can look at it any time. It's running close to the end of the month, the twenty second of Feb. It seems like so much longer, but only two. The Sergeant says go play some cards and drink some beer, Butch, red, Alex were going to play in about one hour, after Alex and Butch get there work done.

We are playing cards and so far, I'm losing bad I've already lost eight Ciggs and only have two left, I quit the game. I'm just watching now, and Alex is doing really good, Butch isn't doing very well either, he also lost a few in a row, red is giving up, he is really lost. The Sergeant just called a mission of ten rounds, charge six, I'm carrying rounds as usual and red is #1 and Sergeant is gunner we are firing about two miles from here, over Saigon to the east. The Infantry is heading out threw Saigon, they are running slow. The Cong is out there a small patrol found them but are not attacking, they are waiting for the Infantry here to get out there then they will engage with the enemy.

Carrying the rounds, I get caught by the concussion of the clash compressor and lost my hearing and my ears are bleeding. Amad was carrying powder and the Sergeant said for him to get me to the medical hooch now so that's where we are going. There putting gauze in my ears with some ointment to help stop the bleeding. I can hear nothing but a loud ringing, they gave me some medicine to calm me down and sleep a little while. The mission is over, and the Sergeant came over to see how I was doing and I told him my hearing was a little better at least I could barely hear him. I will not be able to be in the missions for the noise, but I at least can do some duties, but not Guard.

If I don't get any better within one week, they said they will have to send me home, hell I wouldn't be good for Infantry or artillery if I can't hear. I can go around the camp and go to eat and such, but I am not allowed to go back to the gun until they see my hearing is much better and my ears are healing up. I went by the gun to tell the guys that I'm sorry I cannot help now but that I'm hoping that soon I will be back, the Sargent has me staying over by the Infantry tent until they see how I'm doing later. I know that my hearing will come back, I went to the mess hall which is a tent where they cook the food and they get fed and got me a sandwich and some coffee.

The cooks name is Toni Gaushalas, I'm over burning the toilets and doing some other work and feel pretty good about that. I'm still taking it easy, the captain is ok with me doing some work, but he wants me not to work, but just go around the compound enjoy some bear and relax until they see if the ears are better or there sending me home. I'm talking to this Soldier about how are things going for him, I could barely know what he was saying but he told me he got a letter from his dad, his dad said in the letter that he is rebuilding a 63 corvette, just have to finish painting and install the chrome reverse wheels and it will be done and that when he gets home, it is his that is so very cool. I told him I have a two door fifty-five chevy and it needs a lot of work, but it does run well.

We've got another mission I'm going back to the infantry tent right now, let them do there mission and maybe I'll go back over and visit. I went back to the track. It is mid-day the twenty-eight of Feb. it's the end of another long month. It's the Sergeants birthday, he is now thirty-one years old he's been here for three years and he's been through a lot of hell when he goes home soon he is getting out of the service he's not putting any more time in the army he's going to spend time with his family. My hearing as comeback quite a bit and it won't be long, and I will be good to go. I'm going to pull Guard duty not bad at all. It's quiet yet I thank God for that, the weather is great not very hot it's still in the nineties but it's night now and it feels a lot cooler. In three days we are moving to a compound just south of Ton son Nhut air base and then we'll get set up on new platforms for the tracks. The engineers are building them plus there is supposed to be bunkers built as well. It's the third day and we are packed and moving. Right down highway #1 our favorite road ha-ha.

We will be south east of Tonsonut when we get there. We will be stopping near Tonsonut, the major and captain have a meeting to go to in the air base with the commander there. The Mejor thinks that is a general there at the base. All the ammo has been choppered in to the place we are going so that's good. Right ahead of us is the # one track is lead and we on #2 track are following them and the mess truck, guns and jeep and the ammo truck and then the last two tracks the mess truck is hauling the small cannon 108 and we are moving on a good pace. We are just about passing our first village and the kids are out by the road yelling give candy give candy, we are ignoring them and just moving by. We hear the music coming out of number four track, there playing the (beach boys).

We are stopping for some reason, oh well things are tough when you're on a big highway hahaha. We found out the reason we stopped is because the captain had to tell our Sergeants that they got word on the jeep radio that the small village up ahead had Cong visitors and they may still be there so when we go by the village we will go on top speed, if we get fired on just cut loose with the 50's and just keep moving we should make it by ok, just keep moving on high speed no matter what happens, We've got five miles before the village, so when we are close kick her down on high. The Infantry went through there two days ago, but they weren't there then, but the word is they might be there now. Even if we are not attacked makes no differant, high speed them all the way.

They will look like normal Vietnamese but there will be more of them than a regular village, were moving It's about noon and we are approaching the village God it is bumpy on top, I hope I can hang on and be able to fire the 50 if I have to. We are passing the village, I'm sure that they here these big guns rolling they make as much noise you can hear them over a half a mile away, were going passed at top speed, we are now passed them but staying on high speed for at least one mile and now stopping to stretch our legs and eat something. We are watching closely around us, hoping to be safe. We are done now and back on the trip, the captain radioed that we had no trouble at all from the village and that we were on the move and should be there in about five hours. We see the workers in the paddy's seeing the lady carrying baskets of rice to the hand pulled carts. The baskets look like thirty pounds apiece and they carry two at a time. I all ways think to myself what if there was a sniper in the trees along the road, which we would never see and pick us off the top of the track, it's pretty scary.

The Sergeants are going over to the jeep for their briefing and then will let us know what's going on. The Sergeant is back here I asked what's up and he said there is nothing for us to know, let's move out. I know we will find out later on. Red is just singing out loud it's mumbo jumbo I can't understand a work he is singing, I just wish he knew how to sing hahaha, on our crew is Harold, Red, Henry, and Bill there is two Bill's Dara, I forgot Amad, ha-ha.

We ended up with six on our crew. Sometimes the book seems boring, which it is but it is because it's the same thing over and over, but it's day by day, by week by week, month by month, one Soldiers experience in the hell hole of Vietnam. We about five miles from the compound and we'll be at. I could put a lot of hocus pocus in this book and it may sound much more interesting but that would be a lie, and of course I'm not sure of what everyone said, but to my up most knowledge is as close as I can get it. We are now pulling into the compound and can see the army engineers are still working with there plows cleaning out some more jungle. There is a lot of jungle making up the walls around the compound. The Infantry is guiding us ware to go with the trucks we are pulling onto the platform they built for us and it is just right size for the track.

The engineers call this place hochi men playground because they get morterd quite a bit, oh that's something we didn't need to no there is one hundred rounds of ammo in the bunker and as many powders next to them the engineers are stringing barb wire around the outer perimeter and the Infantry are setting up claymore mines between the barbwire and the edge of the compound. The bunkers per gun are set up with 50 caliber machine guns rather than 60's, they are made from sand bags and plenty of room to sleep, keep Guard and fire from inside with fire holes. We are told that around this are that Vietcong come from the north along the Cambodian border down the ho chi men trail with there supplies into Vietnam supplies consisting of weapons, food etc.

They know what they are doing There is about fifty Infantry around the compound, there is about thirty engineers doing a lot of different things framing the showers and still plowing in the jungle etc. It's now the very next day and finally everything is in place barb wire, mines, showers, and they finished plowing the jungle, so everyone is happy Now all the guys are cleaning up the mess and the engineers are getting there equipment ready to be moved out to Ton so Nhut, the Infantry is just relaxing and getting ready to move out in the next morning. It's about lunch time so we can go eat any time after the Infantry get done.

Oh, hell says the Sergeant, just go eat they will not all go at once, so we can fit in somewhere. It's now two pm and I am on top of the track with the 50 just drinking coffee and smoking ciggs and keeping my eyes trained to the jungle for Guard watch. Nothing at all happening out there but kids flying around and that's all I see. It's going on five pm and red just came over and told me the Sergeant said we are relieved of Guard duty and to just kick back and relax so we are sure going to do that. It's now getting dark we have already had supper and we were told that we have no missions yet, but they are soon to come so stick around the gun. It's going on nine PM and the Sergeant wants me on Guard along with Red and Henry so there we are.

They weren't kidding when they said they get hit a lot we are getting mortared right now some guys are already wounded everyone is taking cover in the bunkers guns where firing tracer rounds and they are sending up flares to light up the jungle red and I are running to the ammo bunker to get more ammo for the 50's in case we get attacked we will have plenty of rounds to fire. We got them, and Red is grabbing the 50 off the rack to get it to the commander's location for them and he's running back to the bunker and getting that 50 inside the bunker, it's all done, the mortars have stopped, there still sending up flares but nothing can be seen now, we are still looking very hard to see if anything moves. I think Charlie sent us a message welcoming us here ha ha-ha. Only to Soldiers here were wounded by shrapnel.

Sergeant yelled mission five rounds charge four direct fire in five second explosions that's not very far, but right in Charlie's lap. The Infantry are not in the way, they left going out into the jungle when the mortars started. They have radio contact with the infantry and the rounds were landing right where they wanted them. The lieutenant is going around the truck telling us we did a great job. Red really put those rounds out good he is a great man we put those rounds out in fifteen minutes. It doesn't take long when you've got a man like Red. We are cleaning up our mess and getting ready, we are done with that and we are going to get eat. We are done eating and back on the track. It's going to be a long day, you can tell because everyone is jumpy, even the commander, major, and captain. I'm off Guard duty and looking around, and the way the commander is shouting at the captain it seems like everyone here is scared that we may be attacked tonight. Everyone is walking around quiet and the engineers are not working on anything, which they shouldn't because there done with their work. We are fully geared for combat, the 50 is back on top the truck. If there is an attack everyone is ready, for whatever happens. The infantry is pulling out to the jungle, that's the rest of them to help search and destroy which will not come back in because they were just waiting for the supplies they needed that were flown in by the chopper already. We didn't think they would stay in the compound very long.

The compound is kinda small for everybody to be here, but to me it's pretty good size. It would be a bad day with a lot here for Charlie to destroy a lot of Soldiers will having a lot more mortars coming in. We are still just resting and eating and sleeping. The Infantry is gone now except twenty-seven are still here. The fifth Mech are coming here this afternoon so that's very good, there will be another thirty men from 5th mech. They're going to supper now, I'm not hungry at all after the last meal I had. One of the Infantry was talking to us and mentioned the tunnel we found in the field, remember where the tunnel rat went down and set those explosions and was telling us on paper what it would look like if we could see them by air the tunnels are like a small maze sort of like finger sticking out of a box which is their supplies center underground. There tunnels are all over South Vietnam, so he told us. It's hard to believe that they are that intelligent to dig all there tunnels, but they did were seen. According to our captain he said that Soldier is right.

We've got a mission, so I have to get rounds from the bunker we need ten rounds, Amad is getting the powder we are set. Well they have started already which means we are carrying ammo between rounds this time I'm not going to get caught from the flash I was stupid last time, but I won't be stupid this time. The Infantry ran into Cong and they want them pushed back so the Infantry can move forward and engage and try and take them out. Along with us. I wish I was out there with them, cause when I enlisted I did not sign up for artillery, I sign up for Infantry, fighting face to face with the enemy not carrying rounds, burning toilets, and filling showers. I put in for a transfer, but they turned me down again ha-ha. We have fired five rounds and told to seize fire. I still do not know how far a round can go the distance. We just shot the rounds one mile, charge seven. I asked the Sergeant and he said quote (who the hell cares.) He is having a real bad day. I ask him that ever so often just to piss him off, but it keeps him thinking of war instead of home.

I don't blame him at all we all feel that way sometimes. Mission done after a while we have another one in an hour, it's just one round every hour, we will be doing this the rest of the day. It's time for lunch, we missed breakfast, well I did. I can't get off the 50 so Amad is bring me some back, it's getting kinda cloudy and looks like we might have some rain coming, the bad news is Charlie loves to attack in the rain, there used to it easy for them to move around better without being seen and set up there mortars, us we can hardly see anything when it rains hard but Charlie can he's use to darn. The rain is not hear yet so all is good, I'm going to get a shower, the only thing I don't like, showering here is that it's cold water. No change of clothes yes wares the same ones all the time, that's so nice it's the dress up of the day ha-ha. We got a haircut here is we want it, if it is too long but you cannot go bald, I did and got loss of strips and a one hundred and twenty dollar fine for destroying Government property that sucked. I was corporal and changed to private quick. Such good things happen when you are having fun. We are starting a mission every hour for three missions then we are done. It's midafternoon I'm not carrying ammo the Sergeant has got me over by the big tent filling sand bags to put around the tent six feet high double thick in place of the tent for the commander to have.

I have no knowledge of what's going on here nor do I care. I have an attitude right now, I want to go home, I have the chills, I feel I'm not going to make it through this war, we don't know how the hell we are fighting all these people here look like Vietcong, children trying to kill you with a grenade, as the kids are asking for candy, they give it to their mothers who in turn give the candy to the father who is Cong, he fills it with poison and they try and give Soldiers the candy. Most villagers just stare at you like they are afraid, you might see a cooking kettle strung on a frame, and below that there is a tunnel, what's up in this country is just pure hell for us any way you look at it. This is what everyone fighting this goes on every minute of the day. Back home you call us baby killers, but the news back there does not tell you those things do they. It's getting dark, there is no rain, just the jungle making the wall around us, oh about the kids with the grenades, I've seen them, right in Saigon. We are pulling guard and as close as we are to the jungle, at night is like a web you can't see a Darn thing in there like you can during the day. This compound has Vietnamese now working in it, they do laundry and cooking during the day and where they go to a night, I guess there home out there some ware.

They could be spy's and we would not no that. They came back every day through the front of the compound, two men and two women, they leave about one hour before dark, four days in a row we have had missions, all the same, but different directions and every night have been safe. The Infantry have been arguing over stupid stuff around here, but no one get mad at anyone, there just very tense. It's now time to switch Guards, my turn to sleep for about four hours I hope. It's getting just about morning and I did not sleep any more than three hours, so I got up and I am taking over red's duties a little early. Red said that it had rained a little about three am but not much at all. I can see why Red is so tired, the rain helped that seems to make you more tired. We just got called to breakfast, I'm not going because someone must be on the track all the time. I'll just wait here, oh great Geronimo has brought me food and taking my place, I call him Geronimo because he is so big, and he is part Indian any way. He is off truck four, I'm glad he brought the food it's scrambled eggs and real potatoes, there powdered eggs but who cares. Geronimo is gone because Red is back. We talk all the time, darn we just heard firing from a machine gun, we are all cutting loose and firing as well, we went through a box of shells, it's all stopped when one guy fires we all fire, that's one of our commands they could have a decoy over on one end of the compound and come in on this end.

The Cong are very strange they will come right at you and give up there lines just, so they can get two of you. Now the Infantry are going out to see, if we killed anybody. We got orders for a mission same as before. They must have some sort of strategy because otherwise they are wasting rounds, especially when they have no idea if the Cong are really out there. That's what I mean about confusion, I just do what I have to do and serve my country. Missions are all over and we will just sit back until another one comes up. We just finished cleaning our mess up It's four in the afternoon and we just got word that the last mission we had was in the wrong place. We dumped rounds on the Infantry, we had no communication or knowledge that the infantry was there they were supposed to be seventy yards from where we hit. They were crossing a rice paddy and had no idea what the hell was going on with the rounds on them at all they were moving in a direction that the rounds would have hit passed them about seventy-five yards away, there was some sort of communication gap some ware. The Sergeant is going over to the Major to talk to him about something. They might hit Ton son Nhut, but there is a very good chance they will hit here, or they might go further south.

There in the deep jungle so it's very hard for the air force reconnaissance to pin point right now, now that we are halfway through the month I think, I don't know what day it really is but close, any way we are getting five men from the Infantry that will fly out to Ton son Nhut and then home, we are getting six men tomorrow to replace, they will just be like we were, but we won't harass them like we were when we got here. Remember when I got in it was my birthday and we went right into battle; God I miss my wife so beautiful inside and out what a Lady. Well back to the war Darn it ha-ha. It's night time in the big city.

It's night and the lights are off tonight it doesn't look good at this time it just started raining real hard and it feels mighty cold on me sitting on top the truck with the 50 I've covered it with a gun cover very easy to get off but good protection from the rain. It's raining so hard that I can only see half way to the jungle wall it's bad it's not a very good sign the mines are set all over out there so if they attack and move in on us, the mine explosion the mine explosion will definitely no there here, and we will send flares up and see them and fire right away. We are sending up flares now every so often, we still see nothing praise the lord. We can see really good with those flares, it's better, we can see a lot more of what's happening out there. I for one is very scared sitting up here rain freezing my ass off with not much sleep for quite a while I can't complain because I volunteered for this job.

There is no movement around the compound it's a good feeling cause it's two am. Darn here comes the mortars on the other side of the compound I can't leave the gun until I am told to the mortars stopped and here they come the mines are going off and there not to the barbwire yet, we do not have the Infantry we had before, we just were told there over the barbwire and to get our asses moving to the front of the assault, they were like ants there is so many these guys are laying over the wire and the rest are running right over them, like I said before they give up there lines for getting two of us. Soldiers are running all over fireing at will. They got a radio call that the Infantry are a way behind the Cong but closing in very fast to attack them from the rear. The commander is with the radio man the captain is out there commanding the troops, the rain is letting up quite a bit there is one hell of a lot of Cong coming I'm looking at the sky and asking the lord for help, I am firing and at the same time saying the lord's pair, it has to work cause we don't have all the men we need to handle this it doesn't look like we are going to make it. I have to get ammo for the 50 + 60 caliber machine guns and getting them to the Soldiers we got them there ammo a lot of bullets are being fired I'm going back to the front, the Cong a dropping like flies, but they just keep coming a lot are over the barbwire there coming in on us and it is now hand to hand combat were fighting them off, hell they have bayonets attached to their weapons, I'm doing the best I can to kill as many as I can, they have got a few of us dead, there is so many of them, you kill one and there's two more.

The Infantry are around one quarter mile from us coming very fast, the Cong now knows that they are coming in on them, we are firing and doing hand to hand at the same time. It's around four am and the infantry is here kicking ass guys are wounded and still fighting, this battle went on all night we are all infantry included fighting hand to hand only, It's simply every man for himself. It's morning and the fighting is letting up, a lot of the Cong have scattered into the jungle, the battle has come to a halt. Seven of the Infantry were killed six wounded one of them got both legs blown off one got his arm shot off another lost is ear ext.,

For me I was out of rounds for my M16 machine gun and the Cong came running to me with a bayonet attached to his rifle. Hell I shot him four times before I ran out of rounds and he is still running, for a few seconds I froze, the Sergeant ran and struck him a long side the head and knocked him to the ground and saved my life the Sergeant grabbed me and said, lets get with it man, and I did not mind at all, they found a few that were faking there death and captured them and brought them into the compound. After counting bodies, we pulled them up and the engineers plowed open a large hole and then placed the Cong into the hole and covered the hole up. Thank god we are going back to Cu Chi in two days I'm so very glad cause you can smell the death in that hole.

The Infantry are going to take full charge of the compound. The way we had to fight in that battle I know what the Infantry goes through and they can have it, now I like artillery well, no need to transfer, I'm going to stay right here, besides all my friends are here I can't leave them behind, they saved my life, all is done now we are either sleeping or eating or just hanging loose. It's a time to think about what just happened the people that were killed on both sides, it's just a very sad time, here it is the next day, we will be leaving tomorrow, so there is nothing to do now except cleaning up the area and putting things back in order. There is a lot to be done now that we've had sleep and something to eat. The engineers are packing there equipment and such to have there equipment and moved out Ton son Nhut in the morning that's all that's going on now, I'm on my way over to the track and just sitting on the 50 caliber, we leave in the morning for Cu Chi. It's time we got out of here, well the getting is good, today is nice weather the clouds are here and there in the sky the choppers are flying in for the picking up the wounded and the ones that died. At least the dead are going to a better place, at least they escaped from hell. Some men here thing I'm crazy when I say why not thinking if you die or not anymore, because I feel we will just take the train to heaven a better deal than this. I'll fight like hell when I need to but not I'm not worried about dying anymore because what happends just happends. It's time to go the Major said pack your self's up were leaving. We are on our way with everything we came with. All the Soldiers are wavering us there good byes.

That's a nice send off, I'm really hoping that everything goes good for them, we are now one hour out and one of the tracks breaks down a rivet that holds the metal strap that goes around the wheels came out or snapped and the strap came loose and we are stopped in the middle of now here until a chopper flies in for repair, that could take a day to get it fixed, but the captain radioed in and they radioed back and said it will be two days to get it fixed. Well they have and fixing the track, so we will be moving in about four hours from now. We are going to run all night everyone can hear us at night better than day because the land is so quiet. Well I'm Guard on the 50 we are moving the chopper has left and they did a nice job and a very quick job, we are six miles from Ton son Nhut, but we will pass and not stop, well move right along tell we get there. We have enough fuel so that's not a problem, we are close to Tonsonut because we can hear a plane taking off, it's either men coming in or men going home or R&R., now pulling in to Cu Chi and it is great to see, it's our home sweet home, the track with the bad strap made it all the way, they're going to fly in mechanics and parts for the track, after the strap is fixed it will be like brand new. We are rolling onto our platforms which is great bunkers and all. Our ammo bunkers need more rounds, but they will truck them in, we have enough for five or ten missions, but that should be enough until the track comes in.

The Major said our rounds are on there way, they will be here in two days, the Sergeant told us to go get some food and get some rest, then later we'll be on Guard duty for the rest of the day and then catch a break and then go back on, I told him why can't someone else take the night in kinda like a harsh way the Sergeant lost his temper and told me you will do just what I said and like it. All right but it's bull shit, the captain heard us and came over and chewed my butt off, so that was that, I'm on Guard. We in the long run really appreciate what we do, red is over playing his new and hearing music from ho chi men up north, he got his radio from his brother back home, he just got the package. All we hear from his radio is propaganda from the north. The lieutenant will leave tomorrow, his time is up, we will get another one very soon, that should be fun, the captain told the Major that the lieutenant is straight out of west point, he will find out quick that here is another hole new territory all together. Well the day is done, and we just had supper, and now I'm going back on Guard, oh good news the

It's morning now and a jeep showed up with a new guy, and it's a brand new lieutenant also we have a man for our tracks three and four tracks, I'm over by the toilets burning them, but just looking at the track, the guy is quite tall and must weigh two fifty he is a big boy, wonder what the Sergeant is going to do with him, I'm done with my job, red finished up with cleaning the track, we are getting rounds to fill up the round holders in the truck, the Sergeant just told me and red to go over to the captains quarters, he wants to speak with us, I'm always in trouble what now.

We are there the captain just gave me my strips back and red got to be a two striper as well, Harold just got E5 Sergeant, he told us to tell Harold to go see the captain we did not tell Harold anything, so it will be a surprise. Our Sergeant is going home in one month and then Harold will take his place, that's fantastic he well deserves the position. He has been a great Soldier, yes know after the captain chewing me out I had no idea he would give me my stripes back, and I plan on staying right with the captain being a corporal is the same as a specialist four, that's what we are, we are called for a mission this time only charge three. That means the Cong are pretty close, we are firing about one mile from us, no big deal, there is more than likely only a small group, I'm off on two getting more rounds, and red is waiting on them, here they are red, do your thing. We must fire five rounds one right after another, the rounds were set time wise for one minute, all six tracks are doing the same, we'll hit the target with a fury of rounds. We are thinking we either hit them or send them running away. The Air force wasn't called because, it was spotted a small amount of Cong, about thirty or forty, I'm very glad that I'm not the #one guy like red every time he fires the breach block comes back only four inches from his chest, then hit opens, he puts another round in, then power, closes it and fires again, he puts the igniter in of course, the hardest thing for him is setting the timer on the round correctly, we all can do that but he is the best and safest man on that spot.

We got word from the Sergeant that we were right on target and destroyed at least one half of them, that is so cool, the Infantry won't have to mess with them there on the run ha ha-ha. We getting rounds set up behind the truck, with powder, it's less to carry later. Red's finger is hurting him, he got in the way of the breach but it's not bad just a little bruised it will be ok. Thank god for that. We are taking turns for lunch. It is now well into March, not much doing the last couple weeks, all the new guys are fitting right in except the lieutenant, he has a lot to learn the way he says things to us, he always wants a salute, we do not salute around here, we just follow orders, he gets real mad at us, the captain just pulled him aside. We don't salute for one thing and one thing alone, saluting around Vietnamese is asking for death. We act as to the fact that he is just one of us. The Cong would love to blow them away, we are in the third week of March and are told that we are moving to south of pliyku, it's pretty cool this time the three quarter came and the fifth mech will be going with us. Near where we are going they had a lot of trouble from the Cong, just a very small battle and they need us there. The Infantry is welcomed on these trips. It's back in the hundreds with no clouds, the more we sweat the more we stink, but what the hell, it stinks all over in this Country, the Cong and normal Vietnamese cook dogs not the kinda steak I want. The next day was the same as always, Breakfast, Duty lunch, duties, Guard, and dinner then Guard. It does not change much but I Harold, Joe and the captain are going to Saigon before the trip, we are headed there now, cool we get to see the shops. We get word they dumped the trip to pliyku. We are going to Saigon to check it out, we have an M60 machine gun mounted on the jeep, plus our own weapons so we have plenty of protection, we are seeing if we can spot any hardcore Cong, that sometimes are seen and around Saigon, here we are in the big city, we can see bunch of stores, we are going down some streets people are all over and kids running at us asking for candy, you can sort of eel that something doesn't feel right, a couple more men ran from us we kinda followed to see if we could where they are going, we lost them but we did see a glance of a helmet, but nothing else we are going back to camp, we see some Infantry walking to our camp with two Viet Cong, well we are back now and everything is in place, the Arvin Soldiers are here and there is a chopper of there here two, I suppose there going to take control of the Cong and fly them out, they are trying to get away but there tied up with rope around there hands so they are not going anywhere. They are flying out, we are just watching there about fifty yards in the air, oh hell the Vietnamese fell out of the chopper, he either jumped or they threw him out, Darn that's sick to see, he more than likely jumped rather than be tortured by the Arvin, the Arvin do that all the time to get them to talk, we have seen that happen and there is nothing we can do to stop it. It's something you never forget, it's a shame they are tortured like the way the Arvin do it.

They should follow the Guide lines of POW and treat them a whole lot better. Now that we are settled in here the captain wants our crew to paint today, where the hell did the paint come from, but we have to paint the shower frames and the toilets black, and after that we have to paint the shack that replaced the Major's tent, they told us, it will be harder to see at night than a white tent, this place is looking pretty good sense the time we were gone. The lieutenant is headed for track four and does not look happy at all, the ones on that track are Al, san, Gonzales, peat, and there Sergeant Bruce.

I hope the hell it's not too bad there one of our best crews that lieutenant is an ass anyway even the captain knows that, he better get straight or end up dead, yes we heard it happened to one in the Infantry from one of our own Soldiers, he simply needs to let up and learn we are not the bad guys, we go through a lot and if he realized it he'd be a lot better. Oh shit a guy just got bit by a 12" snake, the Sergeant there is cutting his leg open to bleed out the poison because if he didn't cut in sixty seconds the guy would be dead when it reached his heart the cut was six inches long after a while of bleeding they put a turnikit around his leg to stop the bleeding they say it's bad enough to fly him out for medical hell he might go home, there are every kinda snack, rats as big as small dogs, spiders as big as a tarantula, scorpions you name it we got them all over. If you look at it, we are fighting two wars one against the Cong and one of all of the above. Well everything is painted any our job is done. It's time for food. It's a special day I guess because we have hamburgers and potatoes yum, I got two.

We never moved out to tri bee like we were going to. They told the Sergeants it was not a good idea right now, we were supposed to have moved out a week ago, It's the end of March and looking forward to R&R rest and recuperate, I'll be going to Hawaii in one month I'll be there for six days, I can't wait, it's going to be nice. Harold is going to the same or day after. We got a mission to back up the infantry that are sort of pinned down out east of here over Saigon, it's going to be a close one for the Infantry because we must fire the rounds almost on top of them that means they are, are on the inside of the infantry five rounds to start and then we will see if they need more. The just radioed they need more so now we are firing with two tracks, five more rounds it turned out great for the Infantry everything turned out just great for us, but now we have orders to move out to tri bee, oh now we are moving like we were supposed to two weeks ago, but this time we are moving, we are packed and, on the move, now we are about three miles out of camp we are going by a village, we just got fired on we are stopping and cutting loose with our 50's we are just destroying whatever is moving they came out taking fire it's an ambush.

Harold is feeding my 50 to keep my firing, all the 50's on the tracks are doing a good job of killing If only you could see you would be shaking they apparently came out of a tunnel and set up in the hooch's and the jungle there for the ambush, remember the last time we came by here there was a cooking pot, they were sturing in the pot but there wasn't any fire to cook with, well we did a real job on the village there are bodies lying all over, men, women, and children, we had no choice in what we fired at because they used the villagers as a front and they were in the same place after it was done we radioed back and told them what just happened and it was over, they said let the fifth mech handle what they can and that the choppers are flying to them for support, and we are to get moving to the only two from our crews that were wounded were Anderson got shot twice but will live to go home Bruce took a bullet in the arm, but it was a surface wound so he'll be ok. I still have nightmares of those children along with all of my nightmares we are moving to Tri bi, we are now only four miles from Tri bi, I asked the Sergeant down below why we aren't stopping at tri bee and he said we just got orders to move on to Monkey Mountain. We are now bypassing tri bee and headed for the mountain. We are short one man remember

Anderson, it will be a couple of weeks before we will get a replacement, we are now pulling into the place we headed for, and it is muddy, just great hardy hare. We are setting up in a big hurry, the Arvin are below the mountain, but catching hell from behind so we have a quick mission, we will teach those Cong it's party time ha-ha. Fire five rounds per truck three powder and timer at one minute, I hope the hell it's not right on top them, but we won't know tell after we fire, no radio back from them yet of what's going on out there. We get word from that they had a handful of Cong, they got them and there taking them back to camp, you know from the village.

The Arvin are losing there battle, but they have choppers coming in with fire power, that will be a great help for them, there fight went on for one day and finally when it was done only lost three men those choppers must have really tore those Cong up, the Arvin radioed our unit and asked us if we could pick up there wounded, and you will not believe what the captain said, he told them, hell no we do not have a truck to spar and call in your Darn chopper, I can't believe I heard that, that's my kinda captain. Our mission did not go well, oh well they called the mission, We are packing up three days later for Cu Chee, We are on the move nothing happened on the trip back, so here we are in Cu Chi. We will stay in Cu Chi tell the middle of April our mission in camp is to just one gun at a time one round every hour out west of here just every other day, we are eating, playing cards. Ken has a camera he got from home and he has been taking pictures of the camp and such, do not know what kinda camera it is I don't really pay attention, we just play cards with some of the guys on other crews, that and just talking of home etc. it kinda makes you feel a little better we are having a lot of fun, an Arvin Soldier asked if he could see ken's camera so ken let him look at it, the Arvin started walking away, ken jumped up and said give me back my camera, and the Arvin said come and take it away has he was going back to his small barrack they have in our compound, ken went for his gun and the Sergeant stopped him and said, let the captain handle this. I'm not even paying attention here anymore we quit playing cards and I'm back on the track, oh great thank' s Major we are moving out to the other side of the mountain we were just here for one week Darn it it's sure short of the fifteenth but we are moving, I'm back on top with my 50 and we are gone we are passing that village we destroyed and there is nothing there but one less village, we are only ten miles from where we are going to at least I think it's ten I could be wrong the tracks don't come with anything to tell mileage so I guess.

We just passed Tri bi and are on the move to that mountain we will be setting up for fire missions on the side we will fire on is the side the Cong seem to occupy the one side of the mountain is full of religious monuments, great color, we are not afraid to fire on that side, on top the mountain is a compound very small but you can see down either side of the mountain, there are Green Berets they have a communication radio that lets Soldiers how many Cong are on the mountain and which side there on, my brother was sent to nam, the Major found that out and they said I can go home or you can let him go home. I've been here a lot longer, he just got here one week ago, and I said I will stay and send him home. The Infantry cannot fight on the side with the monuments. We are just pulling in our positions were set up twenty feet apart and unloading the Ammo and powder in between each track. We are set up to fire but can't fire until the major gives the order. He's got to give us the information we need for the mission, he finally rolled in and is talking to the captain, we are to fire high and charge six number an firing first then two, three, four, five, and then six the tracks are ready and we to fire different direction per track.

We started we will continue until the captain calls it off. We have fired five rounds per gun, we are stopping we will fire more later but now, it's cool off time. Amad just ran over two our track and asked for help, the lieutenant is going over to see what is wrong. There breach block is malfunctioning it does not want to close proper, we are firing again with one less track, it will have to wait to be fired when we get back to Cu Chi. We sure have bad luck every time we turn around, something goes wrong.

We are done with the last mission, we will be here for a couple of days, the Infantry is going to assault that mountain, so we will fire back up and fire on the mountain side before the Infantry starts up. It sure is torture in this heat, it looks like it is going to rain. It's pretty boaring day by day doing the same thing over and over the assault took place and we fired about two hours and we are done, they radioed that's all they need. We move so much my but hurts riding on top the track, we are leaving for Cu Chi and get stocked up on supplies then head toward the Cambodian border east of Saigon. It's a long way from here. We're going, well not yet, when we get there the 101st air born are in that area, that's going to be pretty cool, we made it back to Cu Chi with no problem. We're stocking up and moving out in the morning, we are done getting our supplies etc. We did not put our tacks in place, there's no need to know that were moving. It's now April third and I'm really looking forward to R+R. The engineers are here fixing the strap on the track and having to fix the breach block, but it will take a couple weeks to get the parts, so it won't be going with us. It's morning and we are getting ready to move out, but not down highway one there no road to take, there is still over one hundred men left in Cu Chi, so they have enough that they won't need us.

There waving at us good by so that's very cool we now are going through Saigon, then we will go east, now we are threw Saigon and headed east, It seems like a path, they switched the new guy to track five and we got Amad, the new guy just did not fit in with our crew, it's a hard ride now, the path quit so we are going over land we are cutting threw marshland and pulling the jeep it would have never made it otherwise. The land is hilly, so we are up and down, this whole area us part jungle, rice paddies, and marsh. The Major, captain and lieutenant are riding in the mess truck. We just got radio that what's up ahead of us from the Air force recon plane. So, we are not traveling unsafe. There is nothing in front that would harm us so we are moving in good shape. Amad is telling us about his family he was born in the USA and lives in brooklyn Ney York and Harold said that's your fault and then laughed and we laughed also even Amad did to. I'm glad he is on our track, he has a good attitude.

We see a lot of Vietnamese out working in the rice paddies. We have gone through two villages so far one of them was pretty friendly and looked at us without a frown that is really cool some of the ladies were very pretty nice to see, some of our guys really go wild looking at them whistling etc, we are getting into plain jungle and going through some rice paddy etc it's hard to see what's out in front in some cases, but we are on the right direction, we just met up with some tanks they are going to be with us the rest of the way and there is Infantry with them, that's very cool. We stopped for a moment will the major talks to the tank chief, there telling the major what it is like up ahead, we have been moving three days, so we are going to be here stopped well we get something to eat and stretch our legs, according to the Sergeant we are only eight miles from our destination.

That's really great cause my but is getting very sore up here it's hard when you are taking all the bumps at least it's better to see a lot more rather than riding in side of the track, we are moving at a slow pace because of the jungle, when we get there we will have to dig bunkers etc we won't have showers but we will have the friends we burn yes the toilets ha-ha the tanks are about one half mile ahead of us and catching a little firing on them no one was hurt from the Infantry, and they did kill the one witch fired on them, it was a sniper in the jungle. Sometimes the Infantry can spot them and sometimes not. We are on strict alert, we only have three miles to go to the Cambodian border, we are there and it sure is different it's a little flat land so that's cool, we can set up about thirty feet apart and the engineers did make a dent in the jungle but not much. The tanks moved in first and set up around the small land that is clear, the Infantry already went into the jungle we are finding out where each track is to be, it will take a while to figure that out, at least we are getting the mess truck set up and go eat. It took five days to get here so yes know we are very tired from the trip after bouncing all over on the track all that crap we had to go through. We finished eating and now we are going to take turns sleeping, it's such a wonderful Idea, hah-ah. Oh well so it's not funny.

We are all awake now and digging bunkers. The ground is muddy and it's very hard to dig a bunker when it is so wet, we are digging them larger because all the mud sliding in with every shovel we make. On the boarder is a large creek guys are jumping and sort of washing off the dirt and be feeling fresh with the cool water, I'm jumping to splashing and having a blast. There isn't much jungle on the boarder facing Cambodia, you can see Byson watch us like cows back home except bigger and more tan, they say Cambodia has tigers in there country that would be very cool to see. We are in the area they rains a lot from time to time, we know why we are here, north and south of here Vietcong travel from the north with guns and supplies and sneak back into Vietnam they come down the path called Hochi men trail any way they come back into this Country to there strong holds, we will be going to intercept them at the re crossing. If the Vietnam Vietnamese are Cong and spying on us, we could be in a lot of trouble into a battle that we really do not need, we've been in enough crap in the last month. We have already been in two, we are alive but what if we have another one, I get to make it to my R+R first. The bunkers are done, and we are in the position for the tracks they are twenty feet apart with the bunkers are in between we must fill sandbags for the ammo to set on and powder, so we can cover them with canvas. It took us three full days to do that per track.

We have the 101st Air born are just here off about one mile they are about fifty, so they say they flew in and dropped by choppers. That's great to hear they are so near. We are eating and switching Guard duty until tomorrow, the tanks and Infantry are moving out towards the north but there are a bit staying here. Oh, good news the Infantry just found a trail that they say was recently used, so they are spread out and setting up an ambush if any Cong move down that trail, they are going to be there for quite a while, we are set up good for a fire mission, so we are just chilling out tell something comes up.

The lieutenant came over to the tracks and asked if we would accept his apology and I said hell yes, no problem sir, he said do not call me sir, just do what the hell I tell you what to do. I might be a bad ass from the states but just give me time. Now he is just like one of the guys, cool. We are just sitting around, walking around, I'm kinda nervous about this place, I'm on Guard on the 50 I call it home sweet home. Looking into Cambodia, is just not the same as Nam, there we see lots of open land, it's pretty dumb but if we see Cong in Cambodia, the Infantry gets to have the fun of attack. God, I hate that. We have a mission, long range, firing ten rounds only two guns, they spotted Cong about two miles from the Infantry, they want us to fire to slow the Cong down and destroy as much as we can, for the Infantry so that they can attack and have a better chance at that. We will face the barrels of the truck to the south west and begin firing. We have put out five rounds, red is not doing the firing, Amad is, reds carrying ammo and I'm getting powder, what a switch, it's very hot out right now in the one twenty's is the tempature and no clouds, I'm getting yeld at get those rounds up here, Darn it. I'm not a conveyor belt I'm doing the best I can between rounds, Red got dizzy and I set him in the bunker and now I'm getting rounds and powder, the Sergeant is yelling at me again about the rounds, we finished the mission, and it's going to be one and a half hour before the next one, the Infantry is kicking ass so instead of a mission in one and a half hours we are on hold. Amad is whore out he did not get much sleep last night, so I can see why. He said is scared and that's why he did not sleep well, red is recovered, thank God for that, we are not out with the Infantry, so we are just praying that they get the edge on the Cong and they are all right.

They haven't called for rounds so we don't have any Idea what's going on. But we know what a battle is, we've been there. The Infantry is falling back, we've started a mission just behind them by one half mile, right now red is back at #1 man and the rounds are back of the truck the Sergeant can't yell at me now, I'm handing the rounds to red firing one after another, we have done five quick rounds and we are done. The Sergeant and Harold are very tired, and we can tell, but if another mission is called for we are ready. Darn we have another mission, five rounds at higher elevation, charge seven powder, the barrels are set It's going to be a big mission, fifteen rounds, the men from all the tracks are helping each other carrying rounds to the back of the tracks that way we have enough for each track before we start. We just started firing, we are at ten rounds fired and the flash compressor is turning red, we must stop.

We got radioed that we can stop firing because the rounds hit just right, and they are taking well control of the battle. There were four dead and seven wounded, but that was against about seventy or seventy-five Cong. A lot of the Cong escaped into the jungle and four were captured. There battle lasted six hours, oh hell it just started raining, it is day light, so we can at least see good compared to night. We have been up twenty-four hours, I'm glad that the battle was not here, I don't think we could have survived. We just spent four hours getting ready for another mission, we are getting sleep, eating, now we are cleaning the guns etc. Some of the Infantry is coming back here and the rest are going to be picked up by choppers. Some of the Infantry told us partially what went on out there, some of that was breathtaking, it was that bad. I can only imagine what they went through.

We are getting ready to go eat, some are going on Guard, we will at least get some sleep for the ones that need it. We've been here now two weeks, it's heading toward May when I get back to Cu Chi I'll be going on my R+R for six days, we are moving out toward Cu Chi in two days that is so great I need that R+R really bad. We are here the last two days and we are moving out to Cu Chi finally, we left, and the captain was very happy to leave, he is sick of this place. Well we are four miles out now and passing this little village, they were the nice people we passed coming down here. We are making slow time but it's kinda nice taking our time, you can see so much more, well we went through the trip real well and after getting out of that muddy fields etc, we are back in Cu Chi in just five days we did pass a couple more villages but had no trouble, it was all cool, and the most thing is we made it safe with no break downs. I'm not leaving yet for my R+R. Here we got all set up and feels so good to be here and after setting up we got a mission already crap I thought for sure we would have time off but not us firing one round every hour for five missions, don't ask me why to cause the Sergeant doesn't even know, it's toward tri bee. They say there is a sighting of Cong out in that area quite always about every other week and they had some radio contact with an Air force plane flying over the area that looked like a unit of Cong headed this way, but they weren't sure, but we are dropping rounds in anyhow. They might of came out of a tunnel and could be going anywhere, well I got orders for my R+R in two days, Amad did to, but a different place, I'm in two days are going to Ton son Nhut we are being jeeped there and just praying we make it, there is just the jeep and one mechanized vehicle of a few Soldier of Infantry, we have arrived safely to the check in on the base, there I picked up my orders to get khaki uniforms for my trip, and also my duffel bag I am just shaking with excitement of actually going, in just two hours I am on my way. The plane is landing, we were going to the plane and we were stopped by MP police that the plane was full, we saw these news men with there large cameras going on to the plane, the MP saw that as well, the MP said you are not going to miss out come on with me we went into the plane and the MP told the news people to get the hell off this plane to make room for us Soldiers, I shock the MP's hand and told him thanks, It is may sixth and we just took off. If we would have to wait for another time I would have brookin down in tears. I' am on the plane and buckled up and ready to go and now here we go.

I've got goosebumps we are in the air leaving Vietnam, the stewardess asked if we wanted anything to drink or eat and we did. You can just imagine what I feel like going to America so very cool.

We are now going over the ocean and looking out the window, yes, it is the ocean. I am just looking up at the sky and thanking the Lord for allowing me this trip. We have been flying a very long time and getting very close to Hawaii. We can almost see it is so cool thinking what enjoyment of being on American land oh so cool. We are coming in and landing I can hear the squeaking of the wheels has they are touching down, ladies and gents we are on the ground ha-ha could not help it, it just came out of my mouth. After I got off, there was an Army shuttle to take us to the check in quarters of Army to get my money, what Hotel I was in etc. looking all over seeing American people all over, It is so great we, well I am in paradise, I've now finished checking in and I am headed for the Hotel, I'm staying at the Hilton after checking in and reaching the Hotel I decided that I would like to go see the famous beach Waikiki beach and it is so nice, there is a lady walking toward me on the beach, God she looks like my wife, but I said no it can't be she got closer and it's my wife what a shock pure magic we hugged and kissed I tell yes I'm in Heaven right now with my beautiful wife we have so much to talk about and so much to enjoy we went to the room and just sat holding hands and just telling each other how much I love her and she's telling me what's going on back home, she told me she quit college and went to work at beechnut lifesavers right in Holland Michigan. That's where well live she gets my monthly Army pay plus one hundred and eighty dollars extra for being married she said that goes into savings account for us that way when I get home we'll buy a house we talked nonstop for two hours, then we decided to go the stores and check them out and by souvenirs to have to take back home for her mom and my mom and d, they have a moving sidewalk in front of some of the stores yes you step on it and it goes by it 'self pretty cool and amazing we are pretty tired after the first day and so we went and had dinner at the Hotel restaurant and I had T-bone Steak, mashed potatoes and gravy, I also had green beans, and corn. I had a bear to drink and pie for desert, that was so good tender it melted in my mouth. Now after dinner went to Hawaiian luau it's so neat they have there dancers that have these fire sticks lit and they swirl around there heads between there legs all this while they are dancing, well we have had it for today, just going back to the hotel and get a good night sleep. It's the next day we are going to the restaurant by the beach. Over breakfast we talked about going to take the tour bus around the Island that sounds like a real lot of fun. We are leaving the restaurant and going to the mall to catch the bus to see the Island, it's nine am and we are on the buss, along the trip after seeing a lot of beautiful areas we stopped for lunch at this outdoor restaurant, they serve all lot of different items, we both ordered hamburgers and French fries, this is the life.

We went shopping for us and she bought me a swimming suit to swim in the pool at the hotel, she has hers, the pool was nice after the pool we went back to the room and stayed in for the night. We got up in the morning and had breakfast in the hotel restaurant, I had eggs, bacon, hash browns, toast, and pancakes, man this is so great. They gave us breakfast free because it was our first full day at the hotel. We took the tour bus over to the other side of the Island where the real people of Hawaii live and it was so cool, they have hooch's to live in and they are the original ones, there made of trees and grass roofs many years back that was the only homes they had all natural stuff on the island, they are really cool people, it's a tourist area we can see people surfing in the ocean, and it is so cool. There is an outdoor restaurant with a bar, that is so cool, we ate and drank it was so much fun. After all that we went back. We spent the rest of the day sit seeing, and then went back to the hotel and crashed in for the night. The next morning we had breakfast and then spent time on the beach, there is a restaurant that sells fish, hamburgers, ribs, cold drinks and hot dogs, I got sun burnt a little, this is our third day and I could not ask for the wonderful time I am having with the wife, Brenda, we spent most of the day at the beach we changed in to our clothes in the beach house and went back to the hotel just to relax and talk. We were talking of home and then she asked me about how it was going in Vietnam and I got a little shock and said we are having a great time here and that's all I want to talk about, I said I was sorry, then we just chilled out, I then said whatever you want to know about Vietnam, I will tell you when I get home. We spent the hours before bed kissing and hugging each other and how much we loved each other, I said to her, I have only two days left we were cool with that, after sleep, it's now morning, we went to breakfast, and I pigged out on pancakes. I was full, Brenda had a western omelet, we both had real good coffee, an excellent way to have breakfast. Again we went to the mall to buy some more gifts' for every one back home, she bought me a Hawaiian shirt to where wen I come home, it's really neat, it's a blue shirt with Hawaii flowers, after all that we went back to the room and going to go to the pool when we get a knock on the door, I answered it, it was the FBI telling me we had to leave the hotel by one PM because President Johnson was arriving in the morning and they had to clear the area for his arrival, he was going to stay at this hotel. We packed all our things and went down to the Army check in building, I was going back to Vietnam a day early and they put her in another hotel until it was time for her to leave the end of the next day.

I said good bye to the wife hugged and kissed. The Dam President sent us to nam and now spoiled my R+R. Well I'm on the plane headed back. I was scheduled for a six-day R+R and didn't even get five full days, what a bunch of crap. I was so angry that I did not say a word to anybody on the trip back. I was asked if I wanted something to drink and I did talk, I said no! When they brought the meals, I refused. I'm just thinking of the wife being so upset there a day without me, and that really hurts me. Well I'm back flying into Ton son Nhut Air field. I'm getting off the plane, you do not know how I feel currently stepping off the plane. Two hours later and I'm being shipped back to Cu Chi, and feeling pretty not spending those day and a half that I had left with Brenda really hurts a lot. I'm back in Cu Chi, I'm not saying much to anybody the Sergeant asked me what was wrong, he said you just had R+R. I told him what happened, he was sad about that and said the President should have not done that to any Soldier, oh well that's all done and I'm asking the Sergeant what he would like me to do. He said go on the bunker for Guard, I said sure, that's where

I'm anyway besides a mission or burning toilets. Anyway, that's where I'll be for rest of the day. Night time didn't bother me at all It gave me time to think about all the fun I had and how great it was to see my wife Brenda I talked to the other guy Amad at the bunker and told him all about it, later we I was off Guard me and the Sergeant talked even the Major asked how it went, it's good being back with the crew, I did miss them alitlle.

At least I have friends to come back to. Amad got back soon also, I asked him why he was back before me and he said you were with your wife, but I was there by myself and I said that's your fault we were there, and you could have joined us, he said yes, I know but I did not want to bother you. I said well I never saw you there in Hawaii, but I hope you had fun, well it's good to remember the trip, but know it time to get back the Idea that we are here now and to get back to the war, at least I got clean fatigue's and new boots ha that is great. It sure has not changed here not one bit except the track that was broken down is fixed. Now we have all our tracks that is a great feeling. There is a new bunker that makes six, the Sergeant is telling me what went on while I was gone.

They did not have one mission. Gee I should stay gone ha-ha. The Sergeant said that the Arvin quite always out set up an ambush for the Cong, but it back fired, and the Cong ambushed them. It said that they lost a lot of men but managed to win the battle, I don't care how many they lost half of them are Cong anyway. Well I am back to Rock and roll on the future missions. The next week we had nothing going on but just out duties, cleaning the 50 my M16 and the toilets and truck at least we have something to do. It is now the twenty second of May and I still think of the good time in Hawaii. We have a mission ten rounds one every five minutes over Saigon, they spotted the Cong on route to the South east of Saigon, we are trying to mess them up while the Infantry is moving in on them The mission is stopped after only three rounds, by radio we got the word that the Infantry is kicking ass they just asked for more rounds, thank God we did not kill any of our men, it was close. After the mission we just waited on a radio report from the Infantry, we just got word the Infantry, captured a lot of guns and ammo that the Cong were moving. The weapons were brought in in wagons from the north, the Cong only had forty men who were moving, and the Infantry took them all out, they were five wagons they are two-wheel wagons that the Vietnamese use in the rice paddies that are pulled by hand. The Infantry radioed there wasn't much of a fight. We just heard that near the north of tri bee by the mountain, the hundred and first air borne dropped down and did a good job on the Cong, but at the same time, tri bee was being overrun. It's the twenty forth of May and there battle just ended. They lost four men and eight wounded. Writing this story, you may think that it seems boaring because a lot of things are over and over, but it is my story and I'm sticking with it, it's the truth so live with it. I started writing this story the last twenty years and I get to some parts that still shock me and I threw them out, I take a lot of medicine and see a psychiatrist every two months and he convinced me that it is time to write this story because it would help me in the long run to get fright of the memories out to maybe be more proud of myself for what I did right in that war to relieve the pressure on my mind. It took me the last nine months to write it this far. Back to the war, we have a mission, it's five rounds just north of Saigon, there is a big group of Vietnamese in black silk that they found out there Cong, yes know even the ones in our Compound could be Cong we would not no because in black silk they all look alike. That's just the way it is here, the ones helping us during the day could very well be the ones that mortar us at night. We never know. There is a little old man out behind a tree about fifty yards and he is taking shots at us with a single shot old rifle. He knows we can see him and he doesn't seem to care.

The Sergeant said it's time that old man went to heaven or hell he's only fifty yards, so the Sergeant got on the fifty on top the track and peppered the old man with at least twenty rounds of ammo, the captain came running over and asked what the hell was going on, so the Sergeant told him about the little old Cong was spotted so we fired. The Captain said the rest got away, his that what you are telling me, the Sergeant said yup. The captain did not by that at all. Ok Captain it was me along shooting just one old man that thought he pick us off one by one like a carnival the captain said report to the major, so the Sergeant did and told him the whole story and the major just laughed at him and said good work, now you are going to Ton son Nhut, with you new orders, you are going home, the Sergeant was so happy. He was jumping around with joy, we said our Good byes and he was gone, now Harold is the all-time Sergeant of our track, how cool is that because we are good friends. I think to myself that this war sucks, but I do not want to die that's it, Harold is real happy being the Sergeant in charge of our track, yes that Sergeant that left was headed for the states to get out of the Army and spend time with his family that's very cool, Oh well Harold or rather Sergeant is calling a mission, he is the gunner from now on. We are going to fire one round every fifteen minutes pretty far we are using charge seven we have fired three different times and we are finished it's in the ninties today a real cool one for a change.

We are again and again cleaning up around the track, we are taking turns to eat, the weather has changed, it is now one hundred and twenty degrees, hot. I'm going to just hang around the track. Everyone out here is doing the same thing. Hell, we got a lot of copycats ha-ha-ha. Oh boy, here comes the lieutenant, he is telling us that in Saigon they have a lot of different types of temperature gauges, there different shapes and colors, and if we get a chance to go to Saigon check them out. It is now the twenty seventh of May and we are going to move out near the Air base, we will be very close to the Air base, we are just now moving, it's morning and there is plenty of protection with the Infantry moving in trucks with us. It was a good trip we are pulling into the area, we are setting up facing a rice paddy. It's a bit muddy but not bad. The trucks kinda sink down alitlle, we can walk it pretty good, we do not know if we must dig bunkers the Sergeant just said we will not build bunkers, that's what the captain told the Sergeants. I will pull Guard on top the truck we are all set up in good shape, this time we have the trucks split up, we are lined up on each side of the compound one north, south east and west. Two trucks are facing the jungle, two trucks are facing the rice paddy and the other two are in the middle difficult to explain but like this (drawing) jungle on two sides and rice paddy on the other.

The R's are facing the rice paddies and the J are the jungle. Right in the middle alongside the track is the jeep with the mess truck, the ammo truck is also in the middle. It is now about the end of the month of May and the twenty seventh to be exact. I and Red have Guard duties, which is great because it's the safe place in town ha-ha. Red and I are not going to pull Guard from the tracks Oh I'm sorry the Sergeant just said it is the twenty ninth of the month, I told him well excuse me ha-ha. They have Red and me going outside the Compound about eight hundred meters in the jungle with an M60 machine gun with a radio and our M16's as well. We are told If we see any lights coming our way we are to fire the machine fun and then take our asses up and get back to the Compound as fast as we can. The Infantry is only a mile from us, so If we see light how do we know it's not the Infantry, hell I do not want to kill our Soldiers, there supposed to be on a Search and destroy mission so if we see those light we must figure if we want to fire or not, a very hard decision. We can notify the camp and tell them we see lights, but you know If we see those lights, aren't they close enough to see us. So, what the hell do we do Red and I really know what we will do, the camp just got us a message on the radio to watch out real good because they say that the Infantry may be coming in, how are we to know If it's them or not I' am really confused about this whole thing. All ways when you see lights in the jungle it means we are going to get mortar dropped on us. They radioed to us asking if we are doing ok, we told them we are fine. At least being here for the night, we have food and that's good enough, and we are taking turns sleeping It dark enough that we need to see light just to see where we are ha-ha. Tell yes what we both are scared being out here so far. Red is still sleeping, but it's ok I'm not tired anyway. I've gotten my sleep and it is morning, so we are called back to the tracks, at least there is no mission yet.

You know if the Cong got behind us between the Camp and us we would be dead men If we did not hear them. We are in camp to do nothing but have breakfast and yes do-nothing ha, the Infantry just are coming in there is around thirty of them, hope they have there own food cause we cannot feed that many. The Infantry said to us that the Cong might be headed this way, they said they did not see any, but the spotter plane said they were out there earlier. It's lunch time now and I for one is hungry we are having ham sandwiches and God there good. So much better than the sea rations we had last night now we are smoking to keep calm, it really works. I know one thing that when I smoke I talk a lot. We have a fire mission right out of where the Infantry were at out there where they were at. The mission is five rounds continuous fire then stop we are done and just sitting around like monkeys on a log ha-ha. Amad was number one on the mission he did not do too bad at all. Oh, great Harold He's the Sergeant but him and I are going back in the jungle again but this time they want us one thousand meters hell that's way too far I said and again I was in trouble, so I just stopped talking. It's not time to go but Harold and I have nothing to do so that's very cool. It's really been a long day for us two, we still have about three hours yet before going out, so we are just getting coffee and getting a couple of those ham sandwiches to take with us. It is now time to go out and set up It's still light about six PM. We are out there and set up we radioed letting them know that we are ready. Harold is on one side of the rubber tree and I am on the other side he has the M60 and I have the radio. It's 12;30 am and things are fine. We just heard something our there are I called in and told them there was noise out here but not seeing anything suddenly we did not see them, but they were there about ten yards from us had no time to fire they already we are running by us like a swarm of bees Dam it the Cong. I got up and as I did I got knocked in the head with the but of there weapon and Harold started running to the camp and they knocked him over they grabbed both of us and they forced us into the jungle going away from camp, there is so many going to overrun the Compound. There pushing us with there weapons and deeper in the jungle we are going we had no chose to let them take us better that than killing us. There were four of them pushing us Darn it they stuck the but of his weapon right in my stomach and I feel they grabbed me up off the ground and still pushing us Harold is bleeding, we are not talking because they will not let us, I am about two miles from camp and still walking, not good but we are alive. We must be a long way in the jungle because we are now moving across a rice paddy and still pushing us with there weapons, it's strange that they did not kill us but thank God he is with me I just know. We are going through a village and there are, but in this village, they stopped us and told us to lay on the ground, so I did, and they tied my feet and hands and stuck me in one of there wagons taped my mouth stuck my face to the front of the wagon and covered me with rice, I can hardly breath, but I can. The rice is heavy I can't move an inch. Now that there done with that I can feel that we are moving, I have no idea where I can hear cows and Vietnamese, still moving it feels like a path of some kind because it is not real bumpy.

I can feel the hurt from those weapons they used on me pushing me in the jungle I am being moved threw an area that I think I hear Americans, I'd think they would stop them and check the wagons, but so far, they did not. I do not hear the Americans any more. I'm thinking of red and wondering if he is going with me or not. I do not know if it is day or night. No way of knowing traveling this way. I feel asleep I do not know if it was lack of air or just tired there is only a little crack in the front of the wagon, they are stopping and uncovering me and sliding me out the back of the wagon on to the ground, they untied me and stud me up but I feel down they hit me with there weapons to make me stand up and I did they ripped the tape of my mouth and God it hurt I can see a bunch of Cong and they are just laughing at me and calling me names. They are marching me threw trees and yelling at me to keep going, I do not see Harold at all. I walked about a mile and there moving brush that covered a tunnel they made me get in the tunnel and I had to bend down a lot cause I'm six ft tall, they are pushing me along I came to this big opening in the tunnel It looked like a supply area they fed me after that we took the tunnel to the left it seems like it's at least been a mile or so I hurt so much but I know if I complain they will hit me so I just keep my mouth shut.

Now I "am coming out of the tunnel and they are marching me through the woods, it's all muddy and wet they are pushing me along we've gone for a long while and we stopped, and they are talking but I cannot hear about what. We are going by a place that looks like I have been here before, now I remember it is where I was with the tracks before which is east of Saigon about twenty miles, I'm headed for Cambodia I can tell. There is a different group that I'm being turned over to. According to the sun it must be noon. Why the hell doesn't anybody see us. We crossed a field and back into the jungle I have walked so far, my legs are not going to last for long without rest. Thank God they are stopping in this little village. I'm being fed and having water to drink. I think to myself if the Infantry spotted us they would fire on me to. Well resting is done they are moving my deep into the jungle, just walking and walking has tired as I 'am I know if I do not follow directions and decided to fight that I would just be killed my hands and legs are free, we are walking into the night I'm thinking about seeing my wife in Hawaii and thinking that's the last time I will see here. Just thinking of here is helping me with my pain. Now it looks like Cambodia all I know is there is a creek that really looks like the same way almost that I said before. We crossed the creek and going right so I think we are going north. I can see workers out in the field they are not even looking at us maybe they are afraid. We have gone along ways and they are stopping, they put me up against a tree they sat me down and are lighting a fire and cooking they tied me to a tree and fed me then they were talking to me not to try and get loose, hell I do not plan to.

They are sleeping, and I feel asleep to. I know we are in Cambodia. We have gone a long way north and Now we are going back into Vietnam at least I think we are I'm not sure about anything. Oh, darn I see a Python snake hanging from a tree they are wanting me to go underneath it and I won't they are laughing at me and one grabbed me and threw me forward away from the snake as they are still laughing. Here there are all sorts of creatures. There is a lot of monkeys in the trees. The Cong just shot a pig with tusks or hornes sticking out of his mouth it came running at us when they shot. We are now coming into the jungle where it's hard to tell if it's day or night there thick at the top of the trees. We are walking quite a while it's kinda wet and muddy. We are coming to a camp that has a big ditch all the way around it filled with bamboo spikes with the small bridge we are crossing which leads into the camp the Cong there are laughing at me and pushing me around they are taking me into this large shack. The Cong there looks like a leader he has medals on his shirt. They put me in this chair tied my hands and the chief came around his desk and sat on the desk in front of me and slapped my face and said welcome to my camp. He asked me what my name is and I said I don't have one what's yours, he knocked me off the chair, well me and the chair hit the floor. He told his men to put me in the cage. We were just about to the cage and I said hi to the Soldier that was in the cage and the Cong hit me in the stomach and knocked me to the ground and said you crawl, so I did right into the cage I am so tired, out of breath, no energy and hurt so Darn bad that I just fell asleep. I woke up and the other guy was not in the cage.

I am hearing yelling like someone in pain. The chief's door opened, and they were dragging him back to this cage, and threw him in. He is beat up. About a day later now and they want me to go to the shack I'm going there now I am in the chair the chief is wearing a forty-five gun by his side. I really thought to myself, my hands are free, I'm six feet three inches tall and weigh two hundred and thirty-five pounds I could take the chief, but I am too scared to try. The chief asked me what unit I was with and I said nothing, I just got hit in the ribs by the Guards rifle, then the chief is asking me the same thing, then I just told him yes third of the thirteenth of the twenty fifth Infantry and then I said nothing he is asking me where my unit is located I just now told him none of your Darn business, I just got hit with the weapon again and this time they did not beat me up the two Guards grabbed me under orders of the chief to take me to the hole. They are taking me right now to this four by four hole in the ground I am being put in it now, they pushed me down and put this bamboo top on it and are putting this bamboo stake threw it to keep me in oh Darn it they are dropping a bucket of snakes on my threw the stakes in the bamboo lid I am now screaming, screaming, screaming trying to kill there snakes.

I have been in here with them for about one half hour, they are taking me out of the hole and I am jumping all around knocking the snakes off and they are laughing at me as they are picking up the snakes and are putting them into a bucket of water with a lid. I am not being taken back to the shake and I am sitting back in the chair. The chief said just now have you have enough are you ready to talk and I just now told him, what the hell am I doing here, I am not important to you why don't you just kill me and get it over with, he is telling me no GI you are going to be on our work detail and if you follow my orders you will stay alive. I just told him, ok, yes sir, he is saying yes sir what, I am saying whatever you say! He just said to me, good boy and just told the Guards to take me back to the cage. So, I am going back to the cage. I am in the cage and the other guy in the cage just said I saw what they did to you and I just told him I do not want to talk about it, I just want to be left along. I am now sitting in the corner of the cage with my legs crossed and thinking to myself if I get the chance to kill them I'm going to make them bleed bad and look like pin cushions with all the holes. I'm I am now falling asleep. I just woke up and I am hearing screaming from the shake and the other man just told me there are others here in a different cage. I am rubbing my legs because they hurt a lot. \And I must go to the bathroom and the other guy here said we go right here in the corner, I just now had to go so that's what I am doing the other guy said see those leaves in the other corner those are our toilet paper. After I finished we talked he is telling me his name is ken and I am telling him I am Bill he is telling me he has been here for about one year I am telling him I won't be for no Darn year dead or alive, he is saying settle down we are going to stay right here. In my mind I said maybe you but not me. They are now bringing us food and water. Ken is a marine. I just told him I am Army he said that's your fault and we laughed. Ken just told me that he figured out how to tell time here they give you two meals a day, so every two meals is a day cool. I think of from time wondering if he stayed alive. I see right now a lot of bugs in our cage there nasty, also sometimes we will see a snake, but they do not bother me they just pass through. This pile of our waste builds up ken said and then I take the bucket and fill it up, they gave me a large wooden spoon to pick it up, the bucket I must take to this special hole in the ground, dump the waste and then burn it. And after I get it burnt I go back in the cage. The day is going by very slow, at morning I'll be on the work detail, I'm asking ken what they do on the job we have to do, he is telling me I go out with the other guy in a cage to cut bamboo down and haul them back here, and every other week a truck comes here, and I load them on the truck. and Leaves.

The day has gone by and it is dinner time, I am eating some sort of meat and drinking water. After I just got done eating, I am now doing pushups, sit ups and running in place, ken just looked at me and just told me he may start doing that, I just said I must keep in the best shape I can. Ken said that a darn good Idea, so he is going to start that also. Ken is a man that isn't for the looks of him not very healthy, but I think he will get better if he keeps up the exercise he'll be better at least I hope. It is just about time to be called out for our work detail, but right now they are bringing our breakfast all is from the looks of it rice and water, they are handing us the food yes, I was right it's rice and water. I have now finished and they are taking us out of the cage for our work detail we are crossing the bridge and into the jungle. There is six Guards to watch five of us, us and the other three from the second cage. We have gone quite always in the jungle, and we are coming to a area of bamboo trees. They just told us to take those machetes and start cutting them down, that's what I am doing. We did this for about four hours and they stopped us They just told us to now cut the fresh branches into four-foot sections. We are now done with that and we are told to put them in ten bamboo sticks in to piles of ten and tie them up with the rope they brought with them, and we are caring them back to the camp. We are out of the jungle and crossing the bridge we are told to stop and pile them up near the bridge, so I did that, now we are told to go back to our cage, with Guards of course. Ken and I have been in the cage for two days and no work detail.

The other three that are here are out there sharpening the ends of the bamboo sticks, we are getting fed now and I am eating dog meat and rice and water. The dog taste awful bad. I only ate it all because I need my strength to keep up the work they have us doing They just got me out of the cage and I am in the chiefs quarters, they sat me down in the chair and asked me how things were going for me, is the food ok, are you sleeping enough and if I like my job, I just told him Ok cut the bull shit what do you want from me. He is telling me, are you ready to talk to us now, I'm telling him you should know you have tried over running Cu Chi, you took me as a prisoner and I have no Idea. How that turned out. I just told him you can beat my ass off and I still will not tell you. I do not know, he just told the Guard take me back to the cage. They took me back to the cage.

Now they are taking me back to the chief I sat down in the chair and he just told me, that I was right about noing of the attack on Cu Chi, he just said we attacked and killed all of the Soldiers and that I was the only one that survived, he just said you are doing what we ask of you so If you don't want to do this as well as the rest of your work Soldiers you will keep doing what you are told to do. It's propaganda, but I don't know. I decided to go along with what I am told to do, and I might stay alive. The chief said to his men take me back to the cage, that's where I am now. It is morning and they got us out of the cage to go over to the piles of bamboo, and just told us to take these machetes and sharpen the bamboo sticks to a point and to lay them in a different piles and also to tie them up in bundles I said no I will not do that to harm my infantry, so I did then go back to the cage, where I am now. They just fed us and left me in the cage and pushed me over to the chiefs shake inside the chief said so you won't sharpen stakes well then you can hang and watch, take him to the stakes strip him and tie him up, it's where they have to posts seven feet high six feet apart and they tie you up between them streach your arm and stretch your legs, I was left out here for two days then they cut me down finally gave me water and got me back to the cage, I sleep for a long time then I got up I feel pretty sore but I will not let that stop me. God it is very hard to tell day or night, any way I do not care at this point what day it is, like before ken said we got two meals and then it's a long time before we get another one, so he calls it a day. You would think that with all these lights that the Infantry would spot this camp. They are coming over to the cage, they are telling us to come out so me and ken are right now.

They marched us over to this little shack and gave ken and shovels and now they are marching us over to the bamboo stick piles, two of the other ones from the second cage, they handed us shovels and marching us into the jungle we went quite always out and they told us right now to dig a hole six wide four deep and four long so that's what we are doing just me and ken are digging the others are just standing there under Guard, the hole is dug now they are having the other guys to put the spikes in the hole with the points facing up and now they have me and ken covering the hole with shrubs and foliage now we have finished that they are moving us to another location to do the same, we have finished that and now are being taken back to the camp. We are back in camp and back in the cages, I must clean the crap in the corner of the cage into a bucket and dumping that into a hole out of the cage and burning it, hell that's what I did always in Cu Chi. We can't do anything without a Guard. Ken and I are doing exercise we do pushups and knee bends and run in place to keep us in the best shape we can considering where we are at. The cage that we are in is made of bamboo and a grass roof, the cage is about ten feet wide, six feet deep and seven feet high. If we did not stay in shape to do there work they would shot us just like they did to another Soldier, we saw that, so you know what I'm saying, I walk around the cage until I am tired and then I get some sleep. I did fall asleep, but they got me up to eat. I'm eating rice with some hugely stuff init and drinking water. After I ate they came and got me and ken to haul bamboo out into the jungle again and we did the same as before digging the hole, placing the pointed ends of the sticks up and covering them. Now we are being marched to the bamboo tree again and they have us with the machetes cutting down the bamboo and caring them back to the pile at camp. Now I am back in the cage and going back to sleep except when I must burn the shit in that hole. They are taking me out of the cage to go to the pond and clean up. I just wash myself with water no soap. I do the cloths the same way. After I washed they put me back in the cage where I stayed for about three days it went on like this for a couple of weeks, ken figured out that it was June now. I do nothing but burning the crap and washing in the pond. I am losing weight, it feels like about fifteen pounds. The weight that I lost made me weaker, but I'm still doing pushups and running in place, plus knee bends. We are getting to eat, it's rice and Dog meat and water hum, we know use there shower yes, it's about time and we have soap. I must fill the shower with water Now I know why they did not shot me at Cu Chi, they use us as slaves. Ken has the job of bring the chief his Breakfast, lunch and dinner every day from the cook in the middle of the camp. They do not lock the cages up during the day they just motion up when it's time for work, but they do lock them at night. Now they have a Guard with the cages at night. The other cage, goes and cuts bamboo and hauls them back to the pile in the camp, there is a truck pulling up alongside the bridge and all of us are loading the truck with the bamboo stakes, it is done and now the truck is leaving. The other day they cut bamboo and now they do it every day. They think that they are smart, but I say they are a bunch of dumb Asses. Another week went by and every so off ton they torture us for some reason. With nothing going for me such as jobs, it is now going into July. One of there men was crossing the bridge and was leaving they yelled get back here and he started running and they shot him, then one of there men went out there and stabbed him with a knife. They grabbed the bag he was caring and drug him into the jungle and burned him. They just came and got me and ken and took us into the jungle there was a hole with bodies in it and they now told us to take the shovels and bury them. After that they made us cover the dirt with ground shrubs and such. After the job we went back to the camp and into the cage. We have been doing our jobs well, so they do not harm us. It's been two days now and I haven't had any job to do except the usual ones. Ken looks a lot older than twenty-one years old. Ken has two kids and a wife, and mom his dad passed away before he came to Vietnam, we talk a lot to each other it makes us feel better. It sure looks like this is my home to him but not me. If you think of it all those bamboo spikes that we make, is most likely put in holes all over and there is no telling of how many of the Infantry has fallen in and got killed and it is our fault because we make them. That is a bad ass feeling and we must keep making them otherwise we die. We found out that they captured an Air Force pilot and they brought him here, they moved him out yesterday in the truck that picks up the bamboo sticks. We were told by one of the Guards that they are moving the pilot to Hanoi Vietnam, that's Vietnams Capital. We are now getting better food now I do not know what it is but it sure is good. After days in this cage and now they are having me go with two Guards over the bridge and around the camp to the opposite site of the camp and into the jungle, We went quite always and came to these plants with large leaves, they have me picking them to a big arm full and taking them back to the camp, where they made me split giving of the leaves equally to the cages, that is our toilet paper now, because one of the Soldiers in the other cage argued with the Guard they took our toilet paper away. Days and days have gone by and it is now still July. It's only July but it seems like it's been a year or better. I'm hoping like hell the Infantry and Green beret find this place and get us the hell out of here. But that is a long shot. We don't really do anything now, and ken said it's just the way of life here, and it doesn't seem to change ken has been here for a lot longer than me, he said he's been here for about two years I thought he said before it was one year oh well may be this place does that to you. Some of the stories he's told me about this place are so bad I do not know how he could stand it this long, it sorts of made me really scared knowing this could happen to me.

They just locked the cages up because the Infantry are leaving the camp there is around fifteen of them and every so often they leave and return. When they were leaving I noticed there machine guns were AK47's those are high-powered weapons, I know that because ken told me, I've never seen one. Now that they are gone there is only a hand full of Guards here, one in the tower, two by the chief, three just walking around, there cook and that's all of them. It would be a perfect time for an escape, but there is no way out of this cage. Ken and I will just wait for a better day we are talking about it. Then Infantry just came back, they were gone for twenty-four hours, more than likely they were back with a couple more than when they left. They came with one of ours into the camp he looks all beat up. Wonder where he's from, they are putting him in our cage. He's all bandaged up. The Guard will not let us talk to him, they now are taking him to the chief's quarters. He's there now, he's been in there about two hours and now they are bringing him out and have him sitting on the ground next to the bridge.

There is a truck pulling up, that's the one that picks up the bamboo, they are taking him to the truck and putting him in the back of the truck with the bamboo sticks, we figured he must be Air force and ken said they are going to take him to the north. He is a clean-cut guy nice haircut, he must be a higher command as a pilot. It was at least something different to see. Now they just took us out of the cages and letting us walk around and talk to each other, wonder what's up with that. It's really a good thing I get to study the grounds out so If we plan to escape we will know a lot about the camp, what's ware and who is there etc. My mind was so stured up that I didn't think much about home because, that just makes me very sad and here you can't afford to be sad it hinders to what you need to do here. Days and days and days have gone by with nothing changing, most of the time gone in the cage except, getting toilet paper from the chief, cutting bamboo, burning crap. It's now the end of July and just about August with in two days. It started raining very hard even with the roof on our cage it still leaks a lot. The camp is lit up pretty good, that's another reason why the Infantry don't find this place.

They have a generator so there is electricity here, I wish we had something different to do. Ken and I keep doing our jobs and with our walks we learned who else is here, the other cage has Mike, Jeff, Al they are very skinny and they do not seem as healthy has ken and I, on one walk Mike said he had been there for around two years he was captured in nineteen sixty five he was with the one 144 something but then we were stopped by the guards from talking, we are back in the cage.

They just came and got me out of the cage and took me over where they have there Infantry men and gave me a haircut, then I was put back in the cage, later they took a guy from the other cage. I noticed it is Mike. In a little while we heard loud voices and then we can see they just threw him out of the door and made him go over to the center of the camp and made him get down on his knees and the chief, I can hardly say this. The chief shot him in the back of his head and killed him, they just are leaving him there and the chief went back into his quarters. They have two of the other guys in the other cage to carry him into the jungle, after that we saw a fire, and they returned them back to there cage, that is the scariest thing's that went on here, it makes you think it could have been me. It was Mike he was such a nice guy to talk to, now it's over and I cannot take time to think about that I have to just keep going and hope for the best for the rest of us, I would really like to draw a picture of the camp that I am in but I'm not much of an artist so I won't even try. They now just came and got me and ken to go cut bamboo, it's been quite a while sense we did that it was same haul them back to the camp and then back into the cage. They just got one of the other guys to go and sharpen the stakes. Me and ken are doing pushups and such to pass the time. Ken just went for a shower and haircut; ken and I are on a thinking of a patern that If they come for either of us like they did Mike we are going down with a fight. Days and days have gone by and it's the first part of August, a lot has happened in the last three months. I only take this torement from them because there is no other way right now. We please them as much as they want, and we are fine for now. Because one of us pissed off the chief and now I am picked to go get leaves to wipe are butts instead of toilet paper, such fun.

I've got the bundle of leaves and headed back to camp. Every time I go out there to collect leaves I hear that running water, it has to be a river, but I'm never close enough to see. They always take two of us to get leaves and that time I wondered if it was a one-way trip. There torture is not only physical but mental as well. I delivered all the leaves to the cages and they took me into the chief's quarters, they did not sit me in the chair they asked me if I heard anything from the other guys when we were on our walks, If I do he said it would go better on me here. I just told him, I did not hear anything different from what we usually talk about, things of back home family and etc. The chief said are you sure that's all you talk about and I said yes. The chief told the Guard to take me for a shower and then let me walk around for a while, I'm thinking what's up with this, he is sure being nice. It's now the middle of august and all is well. Ken and I are planning to get the hell out of here. It's been three weeks in to the month and once again I got the Guard pissed off and he opened the cage and beat me with his weapon and then locked the cage and left. and then come and got me took me over to the chiefs shake and set me in the chair and the guard told him what I did and the chief asked me what my problem was and I flat out told him I have been doing whatever you wanted me to do, but I" am tired of putting up with these dumb ass guards treating me like pure dirt and you not doing a darn thing about it, get the picture, he said are you calling my loyal guards dumb ass, yes that's just what they are, then you are calling me a dumb ass because there my guards is that right, if the shoe fit's wear it. Well if that's the way you feel about the guards and my manly we might be able to help you feel better, tie is hand to the chair and his feet as well, now we will see how you feel about us later, get the nedles out, now strap his fingers flat on the chair. Alright stick the needles in his left two finger nails, I'm screaming over and over and crying, does that feel bad ha-ha, now stick them in the other two, I am screaming a lot of times well do you think you would like to change your mind, you're playing games like a bunch if school kids and if you keep it up it just shows me that you are, so go ahead but I do say I "am sorry I will do whatever the guards say please stop, well may bee we should give you a couple more for good luck ha-ha-ha-, ok untie him and get him back in his cage, I'm so sore my fingers feel like they're not there I" am rubbing them in the dirt to relieve the pain, in my mind I just said I don't give a darn now I" am getting the hell out of here. and started making plans to do that. We talked it over and decided that the next time the Infantry goes out on there patrol that there will only be a few walking around and call one of them over to the cage and I'm going to act like I'm sick and I need help, when he opens the cage I jump up and attack the Guard and knock him out give you the gun I will breack his neck there and Ken will kill the guard in the tower and throw me the guns he take off running for the bridge, and after that I am going to kill the guards that I can in the yard and then take me and the weapon and haul but for the bridge keep on running and don't look back just keep running. If we are really lucky we will make it into the jungle.

Ken said tonight is the time because the Infantry have left. I'm really scared it's not going to work I'm telling ken right now that If this does not work we are both dead and he said weather we stay here or go we are going to die so let's give it a shot on doing this. he said Oh what the hell let's do it. We decided when the Guard brings us our dinner he will have his weapon slung over his shoulder, and if I act sick he will come into the cage and when he does we'll act. I really feel that it's going to work my adrenaline is really getting high I just said to ken with the Lord on our side we will make it, I just said a prayer and said Lord if you are with us please kick the devils ass If you see him, ken said what the hell kinda prair is that and I said that's all I could say pray your way and I will pray mine, then I said Amen. The Guard is coming now and I am now playing very sick, he opened the door and came in with his weapon pointed at ken, I jumped up and hit him I actually knocked him out ken just grabbed the weapon and we are leaving the cage and I slowly rounded the buildings and Ken did shot the tower Guard and threw the weapon to me, ken took off running and I killed three Guards I was going to get the other POWs but there were more guards there than I thought so I was running to the bridge and killing a couple more butt ran out of ammo so I just threw the weapon down and now I am running over the bridge, ken already made the bridge, ken got shot in the leg but he is in the jungle they are shooting at us, I'm crossing the bridge and got shot in the middle of my butt I'm not stopping I'm entering the jungle, I'm running between the trees and thick jungle, I do not know where ken is right now at this point I cannot wonder where he is because I have to look after myself. That was our plan go and good luck. I am running until I drop, they are firing at me but I'm far enough into the jungle and I'm hard to hit, I'm running as fast as I can, my adrenaline has left me and now I have slowed up, but still running, I hear a noise like people coming through the jungle, in front of me, I see a large bush with shrubs around it, I dove into the bush and took deep breathing and let it out very slow, not to cause any noise, I was right there are Cong going by headed for the camp, I know Darn well that must be the Infantry from the camp.

They have passed by and I'm up and running, I'm about a mile from the camp, I have to keep going because when the Infantry of there's finds out that so many are dead and we are missing they will with no drought be coming after us, I am at a point in the jungle where there is lots of monkeys in the trees making a lot of noise, which is no good for me, because I cannot hear if anybody is around me, It's very scary. I'm now stopping to get some rest I'm very tired. I am doing all right without food and water, but I am very trained in survival so If I need to eat it will be snake, bugs etc. I've found water it's a little creek and the water looks clean, so I am giving it a try, it's good water lucky for me. The wound I have has stopped bleeding, and I' am going to try and sleep for a while. It's starting to rain pretty hard, I'm looking for some kind of cover, I see one, it looks like an abandoned shack so I'm getting in, It's leaking but I don't care it's cover it's about five miles from camp and I'm praying that I will not get cought here I've stopped quite a while and now I've got to get myself going, I am looking very care full out the door to the shack to make sure I am alone. I am so

I'm moving the same direction I was going, and I am coming to a small village, I wish myself luck because I'm going in. They are happy to see me there acting very nice, they are getting food and drink, they even gave me a pair of there tongs for there feet.

I'm so lucky, one of them speaks English they are very nice they told me I have to go now the Cong are not far from here, told me to go east then north after about five miles I will be alright how cool is that, I'm telling him to tell them all thanks and that I hope the best for them. I'm leaving the village and heading to ware he said and hoping for the best I've gone about six miles and I see nothing but a python hanging from a tree, I 'am going to the left of it and running, I've made it pasted him, so I'm cool with that. It's been a week and one-half days out here and I 'am getting nowhere, I just do not know where to go at this point so I 'am stopping and resting against a tree. It is morning now I can now see the sunlight and it is so great, it's full sun light wow I can't believe that I can see everywhere. I 'am where the guy in the village said he saw, I see rice paddy, and I see traces of people were here, but there is no one here now. I just do not know where to go from here. I'm really tired I'm sitting next to a rubber tree, I just fell asleep. I wake up and it is night time, I'm not going to leave here until day break. It's been weeks out here it seems in this infested jungle. It is morning and I still am thinking where to go next. I decided to go left of where I' am and see where I end up. I'm going past a rice paddy and all sorts of workers are out there but I'm staying out of sit as I move past. I've been walking in these woods, long time and the day is almost gone, I'm eating food I got from the village between eating bugs, snakes etc. I eat there food, it lasts a lot longer.

I've been on the move now for another week and It is night, I've been watching out for snakes, rats spiders and wondering if I will step in one of those holes they dig with spikes, I see lights always and I'm sneaking up real slow to see if they are ours or there's, I'm right where I can hear the talk of Americans, I'm standing up and yelling hey I'm a POW, I'm American, I'm coming in. Some guys yell's what the pass word is, I just said how the hell would I know, again they said what is the pass word. I just said I do not know, and suddenly they started firing on me, I hit the ground and crawled out into the jungle, I crawled and crawled until they stopped firing and I got up and ran, and then I stopped, and said to myself, I'll just sit here next to this tree and in the morning, they will find me. I'm falling asleep I'm so tired. I just wake up and much to my surprise, the Infantry was standing over me and realized that I was an American, they got me up and brought me in to the compound, over to the command quarters.

Glory, Glory, I' am safe, I'm in front of there colonel and I' am saying this, you dumb asses could have killed me last night they heard my voice in American, but they fired at me anyway what kinda crap is that. He is telling me, as he is laughing that the reason they fired is because the Cong uses recordings of POW's and, and they try and fool us thinking they are Americans and we relaxe and they attack, do you see what I'm saying. I just tell him yes, I can see that. He said yes anything that moves after dark we fire on. I said yes that's what we would have done also. Now they are feeding me, getting me shaved, and getting me some clothes to ware, and going to let me sleep for a while, before answering questions. I'm all done sleeping, I'm clean, I've got clothes, boots and even under wear, I feel so, so good. I'm going over to medical, they want to see my body for any cuts, bruises, etc I told the medical officer that I thought I got shot in the but he took a look and said there was a small hole but if you got shot there you would have been down, well I said something hit me as I was running and it was bleeding and stopped later on he said it will be exrayed when you get home. All that being done, I was taken over to the Colonel and he sat me down, gave me coffee and asked questions, I told him about the camp and where I thought it might be, how many were there etc. I told him in one place as we collected leaves there was the sound of water. I just told him that we went into Cambodia heading north then went back into Vietnam and one day later we were in the camp.

Well the Colonel said go and get some food, whatever you want and later today I will be flown to Ton son Nhut. It's night time and it's so nice not to have trouble every time you turn around. I' am now getting on the chopper going to Ton son Nhut Air field, I'm in flight it is crazy I'm alive, well, and existed about being free at last, I have Escaped from hell! We are now flying in to Ton son Nhut, we've landed, and they are taking me over to the Command center, I'm there and they are out of the building saluting me like I was someone special, it is so great, I' am no hero. I'm in the quarters right now and they are asking me, if anything I would like to drink, I said good hot coffee, and the Commander laughed, he said no problem and had one of the guys get me coffee, now that I have coffee he is asking me what unit I was with etc. After telling him everything on that order, then he asked me how I escaped from the POW camp and I told him only that nothing more. He did ask me how I was treated, and I said really do not want to talk about that. He told me that's ok just that you made it out is enough. He asked me If I had any Idea where the camp might be and I said near running water and about six or seven miles in from Cambodia and that's about all I could say. He asked if there were any P.O.W still there I told him there were two others there, then I told him that there were two of us who Escaped the other ones was ken and I have no Idea if he made it or not, I explained that what was the last time I saw him and the Commander said where about did you see him last and I told him and he said we have no word on him.

The Commander said to me well you will be going home in a few days after we finish our questions and we get you squared away with new cloths and such. I just tell him I am not going home I" am staying, he just said are you crazy he also said you are going to do like any P.O.W would do and that is go home and I said pardon me sir but I belong here for the duration of my time because It's payback time, and he said we are not going to let you stay here for a revenge trip, and I told him it is not revenge sir it is simply helping the Infantry kick there ass and get rid of those filthy bastards and he said well If we let you stay you cannot go back to the 3rd of the 13th because they are full up with men, he also said give us time to figure things out and we will get back with you for now just go with the man and he will show you where to stay and get something to eat etc. I just said that is very kind of you sir, thank you. I've been here four days and they just brought me back to the Commander, he told me, If they would let me stay it would be with the 108th Infantry artillery is it you really want to stay, I just said pardon me sir, but you Darn right I want to stay, so he said I think you are really stupid but alright we will transport you to the 108th Arty. I said thank you very much sir and then I went back to where they had me staying. One thing is for sure I did Escape from Hell. From here on out it will be easy because even being overrun is better than being in that POW camp.

All the time I was waiting to get transported to the 108th Arty I never went the Commander Captain came over and got me and we went over to the headquarters and the commander told me we are not sending you back into the jungle it's either go home or do communications here, and I said yes sir he said yes sir what, I said I will stay here and do communications, he said ok that's great the man will take you to where you will begin. I did the job for the rest of the time here but they still had my orders for the 108th Arty, this place got mortared quite often but never had a problem until the Tet Holiday in January, when the Cong attract Saigon, Ton Son Nhut, Cu Chi, all the Military out fit's all over south Vietnam all at once went on for weeks.

I finished my duties until January 15 1968 and then they managed to get me out for home, yes I was going home and I really looked forward to that right now yes I spent enough time here it was time to go get out of this darn battle, the Commander had me in his office and presented me with the bronze star and said congratulations Soldier, now get the hell out of here and on that plane It is now time to go home there is a continental airline plane landing and that's the one I'm flying home in, this is so cool. I' am boarding the plane it doesn't seem real, but it is, it now is moving to the end of the run way and turning around, I sat there for about twenty minutes and we are now taking off, this baby is really moving Oh wow we are in the air. We are flying to the LA international airport. It did not take long to leave Vietnam we are now over the ocean, I Escaped from Hell. It seemed like a lifetime in the air, but we are now entering the airport It is so cool, cool, cool, we are landing right now we are pulling in to the departure hub. I've sat here for fifteen minutes before the let us leave the plane and I am leaving there is two men coming to me to take me to Oakland Army headquarters.

We are traveling in a car, it is so very cool. We are there now, and I'm being taken into the headquarters. He asked me how the flight was and I just told him it was great, then he asked me how I felt and I am saying oh I sleepped in the plane and they fed us etc. he said that's very good now he would like me to go over to the medical building so they can check me over I said ok sir and here I" am being checked out, Everything looks good it's really strange that I did not say anything about getting shot in the lower spin it didn't bother me so maybe that's why, they are giving me a couple shots in the arm a tetanus shop and pneumonia shop and now I am good to go, now I" am going over there to the supplies building for my dress uniform, God it is so cool wearing these and spit shine shoes, looking pretty good. I'm all done with everything and I've got my orders for Ft. Sill Oklahoma and one after a thirty-day leave, I've received my airline ticket to Grand Rapids Michigan that leaves in four hours.

I'm being taken to the LA airport after getting to the Airport I made a phone call home letting them know when I will be arriving and they thought I was dead and said listen you sob my son is dead don't call this number again it took meeting my brother to find out that I was alive for my father to understand that I was really who I said I was they are going to meet me at a restaurant there in Grand Rapids, I'm boarding the plane getting set to take off. I've now taken off and I will be there in no time a couple hours. I've landed in the GR airport and taking a taxi to the restaurant, I am at the restaurant and I see my wife, mom and dad and Brenda's mother what a great sit they were in shock to see it was really me I hugged everyone and told them I love you all and they returned the same, we went in and ate and talked about the flight etc.

At time to go I said who am I riding with and my wife Brenda said, well If you look across the parking lot you can see a yellow mustang, that's yours wow I feel apart with joy it's really mine 1967 mustang three speed on the floor with a six cylinder motor chrome renew wheels Oh man is it nice, black interior we got in our cars and let man this six cylinder is really fast for a six. Turned on the radio, to Rock and Roll and man I'll say you can't get better than this. We took the long way home so I could feel out the car and it is fantastic we are home now I have my thirty day leave the next year at Ft Sill Oklahoma we had a baby, I finished my last year of duty and was released July/ 11/ 1969 we had two more babies in the next years then I had massive problems of night mares, flash backs of the war. I called one of my friends from the War that I new was at Cu Chi as we were talking I told him that I was a POW and he said all we got was the word you were transfer. I end this story now with one thing You Never Escape from Hell end of story.

A proud Soldier.
Written By Jonathan Christopherson
Honor of-William. A. Johnson SP4 (25th Infantry Division)

Author Description

Jonathan Christopherson gets along with people. He has achieved a lot in life after the war, has gained a lot of experiences and writing a book is one of his achievements.

CPSIA information can be obtained
at www.ICGtesting.com
Printed in the USA
LVHW090925231218
601526LV00001B/94/P